GEORGE WASHINGTON

GEORGE WASHINGTON
THE HOUDON STATUE AT RICHMOND

GEORGE WASHINGTON

BY

WILLIAM ROSCOE THAYER

I have ever thought
Nature doth nothing so great for great men
As when she's pleased to make them lords of truth:
Integrity of life is fame's best friend,
Which nobly, beyond death, shall crown the end.
JOHN WEBSTER: *The Duchess of Malfi*, v, 5.

BOSTON AND NEW YORK
HOUGHTON MIFFLIN COMPANY
The Riverside Press Cambridge
1922

The Riverside Press
CAMBRIDGE · MASSACHUSETTS
PRINTED IN THE U.S.A.

TO

HARRIET SEARS AMORY
WITH THE BEST WISHES
OF
HER OLD FRIEND
THE AUTHOR

May 20, 1922

PREFACE

TO obviate misunderstanding, it seems well to warn the reader that this book aims only at giving a sketch of George Washington's life and acts. I was interested to discover, if I could, the human residue which I felt sure must persist in Washington after all was said. Owing to the pernicious drivel of the Reverend Weems no other great man in history has had to live down such a mass of absurdities and deliberate false inventions. At last after a century and a quarter the rubbish has been mostly cleared away, and only those who wilfully prefer to deceive themselves need waste time over an imaginary Father of His Country amusing himself with a fictitious cherry-tree and hatchet.

The truth is that the material about George Washington is very voluminous. His military records cover the eight years of the Revolutionary War. His political work is preserved officially in the reports of Congress. Most of the public men who were his contemporaries left memoirs or correspondence in which he figures. Above all there is the edition, in fourteen volumes, of his own writings compiled by Mr. Worthington C. Ford. And yet many persons find something that baffles them. They do not recognize a definite flesh and blood Virginian named Washington behind it all. Even so sturdy an historian as Professor Channing calls him the most elusive of historic personages. Who has not wished that James Boswell could have spent a year with Washington on terms as intimate as those he spent with Dr. Johnson and could have left a report of that intimacy?

In this sketch I have conceived of Washington as of some superb athlete equipped for every ordeal which life might cause him to face. The nature of each ordeal must be briefly stated; brief also, but sufficient, the account of the way he accomplished it. I have quoted freely from his letters wherever it seemed fitting, first, because in them you get his personal authentic statement of what happened as he saw it, and you get also his purpose in making any move; and next, because nothing so well reveals the real George Washington as those letters do. Whoever will steep himself in them will hardly declare that their writer remains an elusive person beyond finding out or understanding. In the course of reading them you will come upon many of those "imponderables" which are the secret soul of statecraft.

And so with all humility — for no one can spend

much time with Washington, and not feel profound
humility — I leave this little sketch to its fate, and
hope that some readers will find in it what I strove
to put in it.

W. R. T.

CAMBRIDGE, MASSACHUSETTS
June 11, 1922

CONTENTS

ILLUSTRATIONS

ABBREVIATIONS
OF TITLES FREQUENTLY REFERRED TO

Channing = Edward Channing: *History of the United States.* New York: Macmillan Company, III, IV. 1912.

Fiske = John Fiske: *The Critical Period of American History, 1783–1789.* Boston: Houghton Mifflin Company. 1897.

Ford = Worthington C. Ford: *The Writings of George Washington.* 14 vols. New York: G. P. Putnam's Sons. 1889–93.

Ford = Worthington C. Ford: *George Washington.* 2 vols. Paris: Goupil; New York: Charles Scribner's Sons. 1900.

Hapgood = Norman Hapgood: *George Washington.* New York: Macmillan Company. 1901.

Irving = Washington Irving: *Life of George Washington.* New York: G. P. Putnam. 1857.

Lodge = Henry Cabot Lodge: *George Washington.* 2 vols. American Statesman Series. Boston: Houghton Mifflin Company. 1889.

Marshall = John Marshall: *The Life of George Washington.* 5 vols. Philadelphia. 1807.

Sparks = Jared Sparks: *The Life of George Washington.* Boston.

Wister = Owen Wister: *The Seven Ages of Washington.* New York: Macmillan Company. 1909.

GEORGE WASHINGTON

∵

CHAPTER I

ORIGINS AND YOUTH

ZEALOUS biographers of George Washington have traced for him a most respectable, not to say distinguished, ancestry. They go back to the time of Queen Elizabeth, and find Washingtons then who were "gentlemen." A family of the name existed in Northumberland and Durham, but modern investigation points to Sulgrave, in Northampton-shire, as the English home of his stock. Here was born, probably during the reign of Charles I, his great-grandfather, John Washington, who was a sea-going man, and settled in Virginia in 1657. His eldest son, Lawrence, had three children — John, Augustine, and Mildred. Of these, Augustine married twice, and by his second wife, Mary Ball, whom he married on March 17, 1730, there were seven children — George, Betty, Samuel, John, Augustine, Charles, and Mildred. The family home in West-moreland County, nearly opposite Fredericksburg, was Washington's birthplace, and (February 11,

Old Style) February 22, New Style, 1732, was the date. We hear little about his childhood, he being a wholesomely unprecocious boy. Rumors have it that George was coddled and even spoiled by his mother. He had very little formal education, mathematics being the only subject in which he excelled, and that he learned chiefly by himself. But he lived abundantly an out-of-door life, hunting and fishing much, and playing on the plantation. His family, although not rich, lived in easy fashion, and ranked among the gentry.

No Life of George Washington should fail to warn the reader at the start that the biographer labors under the disadvantage of having to counteract the errors and absurdities which the Reverend Mason L. Weems made current in the Life he published the year after Washington died. No one, not even Washington himself, could live down the reputation of a goody-goody prig with which the officious Scotch divine smothered him. The cherry-tree story has had few rivals in publicity and has probably done more than anything else to implant an instinctive contempt of its hero in the hearts of four generations of readers. "Why could n't George Washington lie?" was the comment of a little boy I knew. "Could n't he talk?"

Weems pretended to an intimacy at Mount Vernon which it appears he never had. In "Blackwood's Magazine" John Neal said of the book, "Not one word of which we believe. It is full of ridiculous exaggerations." And yet neither this criticism nor any other stemmed the outpouring of editions of it which must now number more than seventy. Weems doubtless thought that he was helping God and doing good to Washington by his offensive and effusive support of rudimentary morals.

Weems had been dead a dozen years when another enemy sprang up. This was the worthy Jared Sparks, an historian, a professor of history, who collected with much care the correspondence of George Washington and edited it in a monumental work. Sparks, however, suffered under the delusion that something other than fact can be the best substance of history. According to his tastes, many of Washington's letters were not sufficiently dignified; they were too colloquial, they even let slip expressions which no man conscious that he was the model of propriety, the embodiment of the dignity of history, could have used. So Mr. Sparks without blushing went through Washington's letters and substituted for the originals words which he decided were more seemly. Again the public came to know George Washington, not by his own words, but by those attributed to him by an overzealous stylist-pedant.

Well might the Father of his Country pray to be delivered from the parsons.

One of the earliest records of Washington's youth is the copy, written in his beautiful, almost copperplate hand, of "Rules of Civility & Decent Behavior, In Company and Conversation." These maxims were taken from an English book called "The Young Man's Companion," by W. Mather. It had passed through thirteen editions and contained information upon many matters besides conduct. Perhaps Washington copied the maxims as a school exercise; perhaps he learned them by heart.

They are for the most part the didactic aphorisms which greatly pleased our worthy ancestors during the middle of the eighteenth century and later. Some of the entries referred to simple matters of deportment: you must not turn your back on persons to whom you talk. Others touch morals rather than manners. One imagines that the parson or elderly uncles allowed themselves to bestow this indisputably correct advice upon the youths whom they were interested in. A boy brought up rigidly on these doctrines could hardly fail to become a prig unless he succeeded in following the last injunction of all: "Labor to keep alive in your heart, that little spark of celestial fire called conscience."

When he was twelve years old, Washington's

father died, and his older half-brother, Lawrence, who inherited the estate now known as Mount Vernon, became his guardian. Lawrence had married the daughter of a neighbor, Lord Fairfax, who owned one of the largest estates in Virginia. Fairfax and he had served in the Navy at Cartagena under Admiral Vernon, from whom the Washington manor took its name. The Lord wished to have his domain surveyed and he offered George the work of surveying it. George, then a sturdy lad of seventeen, accepted gladly, and for more than two years he carried it on. The Fairfax estate extended far into the west, beyond the immediate tidewater district, beyond the fringe of sparsely settled clearings, into the wilderness itself. The effect of his experience as surveyor lasted throughout George Washington's life. His self-reliance and his courage never flagged. Sometimes he went alone and passed weeks among the solitudes; sometimes he had a companion whom he had to care for as well as for himself. But besides the toughening of his character which this pioneer life assured him, he got much information, which greatly influenced, years later, his views on the development, not only of Virginia, but of the Northwest. Perhaps from this time there entered into his heart the conviction that the strongest bond of union must sometime bind together the various colonies, so different in resources and in interests, including his native commonwealth.

From journals kept during some of his expeditions we see that he was a clear observer and an accurate reporter; far from bookish, but a careful penman, and conscious of the obligation laid upon him to acquire at least the minimum of polite knowledge which was expected of a country gentleman such as he aspired to be.

Here is an extract in which he describes the squalid conditions under which he passed some of his life as a woodsman and surveyor.

We got our suppers and was lighted into a Room and I not being so good a woodsman as ye rest of my company, striped myself very orderly and went into ye Bed, as they calld it, when to my surprize, I found it to be nothing but a little straw matted together without sheets or any thing else, but only one thread bare blanket with double its weight of vermin, such as Lice, Fleas, etc. I was glad to get up (as soon as ye light was carried from us). I put on my cloths and lay as my companions. Had we not been very tired, I am sure we should not have slep'd much that night. I made a Promise not to sleep so from that time forward, chusing rather to sleep in ye open air before a fire, as will appear hereafter.

Wednesday 16th. We set out early and finish'd about one o'clock and then Travelled up to Frederick Town, where our Baggage came to us. We cleaned ourselves (to get rid of ye game we had catched ye night before). I took a Review of ye Town and then return'd to our

Lodgings where we had a good Dinner prepared for us.
Wine and Rum Punch in plenty, and a good Feather Bed
with clean sheets, which was a very agreeable regale.

The longest of Washington's early expeditions was
the "Journey over the Mountains, began Fryday
the 11th of March 1747/8." The mountains were
the Alleghanies, and the trip gave him a closer acquaintance than he had had with Indians in the
wilds. On his return, he stayed with his half-brother,
Lawrence, at Mount Vernon, or with Lord Fairfax,
and enjoyed the country life common to the richer
Virginians of the time. Towns which could provide
an inn being few and far between, travellers sought
hospitality in the homes of the well-to-do residents,
and every one was in a way a neighbor of the other
dwellers in his county. So both at Belvoir and at
Mount Vernon, guests were frequent and broke the
monotony and loneliness of their inmates. I think
the reputation of gravity, which was fixed upon
Washington in his mature years, has been projected
back over his youth. The actual records are lacking,
but such hints and surmises as we have do not warrant our thinking of him as a self-centred, unsociable
youth. On the contrary, he was rather, what would
be called now, a sport, ready for hunting or riding,
of splendid physical build, agile and strong. He
liked dancing, and was not too shy to enjoy the so-

ciety of young women; indeed, he wrote poems to some
of them, and seems to have been popular with them.
And still, the legend remains that he was bashful.

From our earliest glimpses of him, Washington
appears as a youth very particular as to his dress.
He knew how to rough it as the extracts of his personal journals which I have quoted show, and this
passage confirms:

I seem to be in a place where no real satisfaction is to
be had. Since you received my letter in October last,
I have not sleep'd above three or four nights in a bed,
but, after walking a good deal all the day, I lay down
before the fire upon a little hay, straw, fodder, or bear-
skin, which ever is to be had, with man, wife, and children, like a parcel of dogs and cats, and happy is he who
gets the berth nearest the fire. There's nothing would
make it pass off tolerably but a good reward. A dou-
bloon is my constant gain every day that the weather
will permit my going out, and sometimes six pistoles.
The coldness of the weather will not allow of my making
a long stay, as the lodging is rather too cold for this time
of year. I have never had my clothes off but lay and
sleep in them, except the few nights I have lay'n in
Frederic Town.[1]

Later, when Washington became master of Mount
Vernon, his servants were properly liveried. He himself rode to hounds in the approved apparel of a fox-
hunting British gentleman, and we find in the lists
of articles for which he sends to London the names

[1] Hapgood, p. 11.

of clothes and other articles for Mrs. Washington and the children carefully specified with the word "fashionable" or "very best quality" added. Still later, when he was President he attended to this matter of dress with even greater punctilio.

One incident of this early period should not be passed by unmentioned. Admiral Vernon offered him an appointment as midshipman in the navy, but Washington's mother objected so strongly that Washington gave up the opportunity. We may well wonder whether, if he had accepted it, his career might not have been permanently turned aside. Had he served ten or a dozen years in the navy, he might have grown to be so loyal to the King, that, when the Revolution came, he would have been found in command of one of the King's men-of-war, ordered to put down the Rebels in Boston, or in New York. Thus Fate suggests amazing alternatives to us in the retrospect, but in the actual living, Fate makes it clear that the only course which could have happened was that which did happen.

In 1751 the health of Washington's brother, Lawrence, became so bad from consumption that he decided to pass the winter in a warm climate. He chose the Island of Barbados, and his brother George accompanied him. Shortly before sailing, George was commissioned one of the Adjutants-General of

Virginia, with the rank of Major, and the pay of £150 a year. They sailed on the Potomac River, perhaps near Mount Vernon, on September 28, 1751, and landed at Bridgetown on November 3d. The next day they were entertained at breakfast and dinner by Major Clark, the British officer who commanded some of the fortifications of the island.' "We went," says George Washington, in a journal he kept, "myself with some reluctance, as the smallpox was in his family." Thirteen days later, George fell ill of a very strong case of smallpox which kept him housed for six weeks and left his face much disfigured for life with pock marks, a fact which, so far as I have observed his portraits, the painters have carefully forgotten to indicate.

The brothers passed a fairly pleasant month and a half at the Barbados. Major Clark, and other gentlemen and officials of the island, showed them much attention. They enjoyed the hospitality of the Beefsteak and Tripe Club, which seems to have been the fashionable club. On one occasion, Washington was taken to the play to see the "Tragedy of George Barnwell." This may have been the first time that he went to the theatre. He refers to it in his journal with his habitual caution:

Was treated with a play ticket by Mr. Carter to see the Tragedy of George Barnwell acted: the character of

Barnwell and several others was said to be well per-form'd there was Musick a Dapted and regularly con-ducted by Mr.

But Lawrence Washington's consumption did not improve: he grew homesick and pined for his wife and for Mount Vernon. The physicians had recom-mended him to spend a full year at Barbados, in order to give the climate and the regimen there a fair trial, but he could not endure it longer, and, with his brother George's approval, he set sail for Virginia, on the twenty-second of December, 1751. On the fourth day of the following March, George reached his brother Augustine's at Wakefield. Even from his much-mutilated journal, we can see that he travelled with his eyes open, and that his interests were many. As he mentioned in his journal thirty persons with whom he became acquainted at the Barbados, we infer that in spite of bashfulness he was an easy mixer. This short journey to the Bar-bados marks the only occasion on which George Washington went outside of the borders of the American Colonies, which became later, chiefly through his genius, the United States. [1]

In July, 1752, Lawrence Washington died of the disease which he had long struggled against. He

[1] J. M. Toner: *The Daily Journal of Major George Washington in 1751–2* (Albany, N.Y., 1892).

left his fortune and his property, including Mount
Vernon, to his daughter, Mildred, and he appointed
his brother, George, her guardian. She was a sweet-
natured girl, but very frail, who died before long,
probably of the same disease which had carried her
father off, and, until its infectious nature was understood, used to decimate families from generation to
generation.

To have thrust upon him, at the age of twenty,
the management of a large estate might seem a
heavy burden for any young man; but George Washington was equal to the task, and it seems as if much
of his career up to that time was a direct preparation
for it. He knew every foot of its fields and meadows,
of its woodlands and streams; he knew where each
crop grew, and its rotation; he had taken great interest in horses and cattle, and in the methods for
maintaining and improving their breed; and now, of
course being master, his power of choosing good men
to do the work was put to the test. But he had not
been long at these new occupations before public
duties drew him away from them.

Though they knew it not, the European settlers in North America were approaching a life-and-
death catastrophe. From the days when the English
and the French first settled on the continent, Fate
ordained for them an irrepressible conflict. Should

France prevail? Should England prevail? With the growth of their colonies, both the English and the French felt their rivalry sharpened. Although distances often very broad kept them apart in space, yet both nations were ready to prove the terrible truth that when two men, or two tribes, wish to fight each other, they will find out a way. The French, at New Orleans, might be far away from the English at Boston; and the English, in New York, or in Philadelphia, might be removed from the French in Quebec; but in their hatreds they were near neighbors. The French pushed westward along the St. Lawrence to the Great Lakes, and from Lake Erie, they pushed southward, across the rich plains of Ohio, to the Ohio River. Their trails spread still farther into the Western wilderness. They set up trading-posts in the very region which the English settlers expected to occupy in the due process of their advance. At the junction of the Monongahela and Ohio Rivers, they planted Fort Duquesne, which not only commanded the approach to the territory through which the Ohio flowed westward, but served notice on the English that the French regarded themselves as the rightful claimants of that territory.

In 1753 Governor Dinwiddie, of Virginia, had sent a commissioner to warn the French to cease from encroaching on the lands in the Ohio wilderness which belonged to the King of England, but the messenger stopped one hundred and fifty miles short of his goal. Therefore, the Governor decided to despatch another envoy. He selected George Washington, who was already well known for his surveying, and for his expedition beyond the mountains, and doubtless had the backing of the Fairfaxes and other influential gentlemen. Washington set out on the same day he received his appointment from Governor Dinwiddie (October 31, 1753), engaged Jacob Van Braam, a Hollander who had taught him fencing, to be his French interpreter; and Christopher Gist, the best guide through the Virginia wilderness, to pilot the party. In spite of the wintry conditions which beset them, they made good time. Washington presented his official warning to M. Joncaire, the principal French commander in the region under dispute, but he replied that he must wait for orders from the Governor in Quebec. One object of Washington's mission was to win over, if possible, the Indians, whose friendship for either the French or the English depended wholly on self-interest. He seems to have been most successful in securing the friendship of Thanacarishon, the great Seneca Chief, known as the Half-King. This native left it as his opinion that the colonel was a good-natured man, but had no experience; he took upon him to command the Indians as his slaves, and would have them every day upon the scout and to attack the enemy by themselves, but would by no means take advice from the Indians. He lay in one place from one full moon to the other, without making any fortifications, except that little thing on the meadow, whereas, had he taken advice, and built such fortifications as I advised him, he might easily have beat off the French. But the French in the engagement acted like cowards, and the English like fools.[1]

Believing that he could accomplish no more at that time, Washington retraced his steps and returned to Williamsburg.

Governor Dinwiddie, being much disappointed with the outcome of the expedition, urged the Virginian Legislature to equip another party sufficiently strong to be able to capture Fort Duquesne, and to confirm the British control of the Ohio. The Burgesses, however, pleaded economy, and refused to grant funds adequate to this purpose. Nevertheless, the Governor having equipped a small troop, under the command of Colonel Fry, with Washington as second, hurried it forth. During May and June they were near the Forks, and with the approach of danger, Washington's spirit and recklessness increased. In a slight skirmish, M. de Jumonville, the French commander, was killed. Fry died of disease and

[1] Quoted by Lodge, I, 74.

Washington took his place as commander. Perceiving that his own position was precarious, and expecting an attack by a large force of the enemy, he entrenched himself near Great Meadows in a hastily built fort, which he called Fort Necessity, and thought it possible to defend, even with his own small force, against five hundred French and Indians. He miscalculated, however. The enemy exceeded in numbers all his expectations. His own resources dwindled; and so he took the decision of a practical man and surrendered the fort, on condition that he and his men be allowed to march out with the honors of war. They returned to Virginia with little delay.

The Burgesses and the people of the State, though chagrined, did not take so gloomy a view of the collapse of the expedition as Washington himself did. His own depression equalled his previous exaltation. As he thought over the affairs of the past half-year in the quiet of Mount Vernon, the feeling which he had had from the start, that the expedition had not been properly planned, or directed, or reënforced in men and supplies, was confirmed. Governor Dinwiddie's notion that raw volunteers would suffice to overcome trained soldiers had been proved a delusion. The inadequate pay and provisions of the officers irritated Washington, not only because they were insufficient, but also because they fell far short of those of the English regulars.

In his penetrating Biography of Washington, Senator Lodge regards his conduct of the campaign, which ended in the surrender of Great Meadows, and his narrative as revealing Washington as a "profoundly silent man." Carlyle, Senator Lodge says, who preached the doctrine of silence, brushed Washington aside as a "bloodless Cromwell," "failing utterly to see that he was the most supremely silent of the great men of action that the world can show." Let us admit the justice of the strictures on Carlyle, but let us ask whether Washington's letters at this time spring from a "silent" man. He writes with perfect openness to Governor Dinwiddie; complains of the military system under which the troops are paid and the campaign is managed; he repeatedly condemns the discrimination against the Virginian soldiers in favor of the British regulars; and he points out that instead of attempting to win the popularity of the Virginians, they are badly treated. Their rations are poor, and he reminds the Governor that a continuous diet of salt pork and water does not inspire enthusiasm in either the stomach or the spirit. No wonder that the officers talk of resigning. "For my own part I can answer, I have a constitution hardy enough to encounter and undergo the most severe

trials, and, I flatter myself, resolution to face what
any man durst, as shall be proved when it comes to
the test, which I believe we are on the borders of."
In several other passages from letters at this time,
we come upon sentiments which indicate that Washington had at least a sufficiently high estimation of
his own worth, and that his genius for silence had
not yet curbed his tongue. There is the famous boast
attributed to him by Horace Walpole. In a despatch
which Washington sent back to the Governor after
the little skirmish in which Jumonville was killed,
Washington said: "'I heard the bullets whistle, and,
believe me, there is something charming in the sound.'
On hearing of this the King said sensibly, 'he would
not say so if he had been used to hear many.'"
This reply of George II deserves to be recorded if
only because it is one of the few feeble witticisms
credited to the Hanoverian Kings. Years afterward,
Washington declared that he did not remember ever
having referred to the charm of listening to whistling
bullets. Perhaps he never said it; perhaps he forgot.
He was only twenty-two at the time of the Great
Meadows campaign. No doubt he was as well aware
as was Governor Dinwiddie, and other Virginians,
that he was the best equipped man on the expedition,
experienced in actual fighting, and this, added to his
qualifications as a woodsman, had given him a real

zest for battle. In their discussion over the camp-fire, he and his fellow officers must inevitably have criticized the conduct of the expedition, and it may well be that Washington sometimes insisted that if his advice were followed things would go better. Not on this account, therefore, must we lay too much blame on him for being conceited or immodest. He knew that he knew, and he did not dissemble the fact. Silence came later.

The result of the expeditions to and skirmishes at the Forks of the Ohio was that England and France were at war, although they had not declared war on each other. A chance musket shot in the backwoods of Virginia started a conflict which reverberated in Europe, disturbed the peace of the world for seven years, and had serious consequences in the French and English colonies of North America. The news of Washington's disaster at Fort Necessity aroused the British Government to the conclusion that it must make a strong demonstration in order to crush the swelling prestige of the French rivals in America. The British planned, accordingly, to send out three expeditions, one against Fort Duquesne, another against the French in Nova Scotia, and a third against Quebec. The command of the first they gave to General Edward Braddock. He was then sixty years old, had been in the Regular Army all his life, had served in Holland, at L'Orient, and at Gibraltar, was a brave man, and an almost fanatical believer in the rules of war as taught in the manuals. During the latter half of 1754, Governor Dinwiddie was endeavoring against many obstacles to send another expedition, equipped by Virginia herself, to the Ohio. Only in the next spring, however, after Braddock had come over from England with a relatively large force of regulars, were the final preparations for a campaign actually made. Washington, in spite of being the commander-in-chief of the Virginia forces, had his wish of going as a volunteer at his own expense. He wrote his friend William Byrd, on April 20, 1755, from Mount Vernon:

I am now preparing for, and shall in a few days set off, to serve in the ensuing campaign, with different views, however, from those I had before. For here, if I can gain any credit, or if I am entitled to the least countenance and esteem, it must be from serving my country without fee or reward; for I can truly say, I have no expectation of either. To merit its esteem, and the good will of my friends, is the sum of my ambition, having no prospect of attaining a commission, being well assured it is not in Gen'l Braddock's power to give such an one as I would accept of. The command of a Company is the highest commission vested in his gift. He was so obliging as to desire my company this campaign, has honoured me with particular marks of his esteem, and kindly invited me into his family — a circumstance which will ease me of expences that otherwise must have accrued in furnishing stores, camp equipages, etc.

Whereas the cost will now be easy (comparatively speaking), as baggage, horses, tents, and some other necessaries, will constitute the whole of the charge.[1]

The army began to move about the middle of May, but it went very slowly. During June Washington was taken with an acute fever, in spite of which he pressed on, but he became so weak that he had to be carried in a cart, as he was unable to sit his horse. Braddock, with the main army, had gone on ahead, and Washington feared that the battle, which he believed imminent, would be fought before he came up with the front. But he rejoined the troops on July 8th. The next day they forded the Monongahela and proceeded to attack Fort Duquesne. Writing from Fort Cumberland, on July 18th, Washington gave Governor Dinwiddie the following account of Braddock's defeat. The one thing happened which Washington had felt anxious about — a surprise by the Indians. He had more than once warned Braddock of this danger, and Benjamin Franklin had warned him too before the expedition started, but Braddock, with perfect British contempt, had replied that though savages might be formidable to raw Colonials, they could make no impression on disciplined troops. The surprise came and thus Washington reports it:

[1] Ford, I, 148–49.

When we came to this place, we were attacked (very unexpectedly) by about three hundred French and Indians. Our numbers consisted of about thirteen hundred well armed men, chiefly Regulars, who were immediately struck with such an inconceivable panick, that nothing but confusion and disobedience of orders prevailed among them. The officers, in general, behaved with incomparable bravery, for which they greatly suffered, there being near 60 killed and wounded — a large proportion, out of the number we had!

The Virginia companies behaved like men and died like soldiers; for I believe out of three companies that were on the ground that day scarce thirty were left alive. Capt. Peyroney and all his officers, down to a corporal, were killed; Capt. Polson had almost as hard a fate, for only one of his escaped. In short, the dastardly behaviour of the Regular troops (so-called) exposed those who were inclined to do their duty to almost certain death; and, at length, in despite of every effort to the contrary, broke and ran as sheep before hounds, leaving the artillery, ammunition, provisions, baggage, and, in short, everything a prey to the enemy. And when we endeavored to rally them, in hopes of regaining the ground and what we had left upon it, it was with as little success as if we had attempted to have stopped the wild bears of the mountains, or rivulets with our feet; for they would break by, in despite of every effort that could be made to prevent it.

The General was wounded in the shoulder and breast, of which he died three days after; his two aids-de-camp were both wounded, but are in a fair way of recovery; Colo. Burton and Sr. John St. Clair are also wounded, and I hope will get over it; Sir Peter Halket, with many other brave officers, were killed in the field. It is supposed that we had three hundred or more killed; about that number we brought off wounded, and it is conjectured (I believe with much truth) that two thirds of both received their shot from our own cowardly Regulars, who gathered themselves into a body, contrary to orders, ten or twelve deep, would then level, fire and shoot down the men before them.[1]

In this admirable letter Washington tells nothing about his own prowess in the battle, where he rode to all parts of the field, trying to stem the retreat, and had two horses shot under him and four bullet holes in his coat. He tried to get the troops to break ranks and to screen themselves behind rocks and trees, but Braddock, helpless without his rules, drove them back to regular formation with the flat of his sword, and made them an easy mark for the volleys of the enemy. Washington's personal valor could not fail to be admired, although his audacity exposed him to unjustified risks.

On reaching Fort Cumberland he wrote to his brother John, on July 18th:

As I have heard, since my arrival at this place, a circumstantial account of my death and dying speech, I take this early opportunity of contradicting the first, and assuring you, that I have not as yet composed the latter. But, by the all-powerful dispensations of Providence, I have been protected beyond all human probability and expectation.[2]

The more he thought over the events of that day, the more was he amazed — "I join very heartily

[1] Ford, I, 173–74–75.　　[2] Ibid., 175–76.

with you in believing," he wrote Robert Jackson on
August 2d, "that when this story comes to be re-
lated in future annals, it will meet with unbelief and
indignation, for had I not been witness to the fact
on that fatal day, I should scarce have given credit
to it even *now*."[1]

Although Washington was thoroughly disgusted
by the mismanagement of military affairs in Virginia,
he was not ready to deny the appeals of patriotism.
From Mount Vernon, on August 14, 1755, he wrote
his mother:

HONORED MADAM, If it is in my power to avoid going
to the Ohio again, I shall; but if the command is pressed
upon me, by the general *voice* of the country, and offered
upon such terms as cannot be objected against, it would
reflect dishonor upon me to refuse; and *that*, I am sure
must or *ought* to give you greater uneasiness, than my
going in an honorable command, for upon no other
terms I will accept of it. At present I have no proposals
made to me, nor have I any advice of such an intention,
except from private hands.[2]

Braddock's defeat put an end to campaigning in
Virginia for some time. The consternation it caused,
not only held the people of the sparse western settlements in alarm but agitated the tidewater towns
and villages. The Burgesses and many of the inhabitants had not yet learned their lesson sufficiently
to set about reorganizing their army system, but the

[1] Ford, I, 177.   [2] *Ibid.*, 180–81.

Assembly partially recognized its obligation to the men who had fought by voting to them a small sum for losses during their previous service. Washington received £300, but his patriotic sense of duty kept him active. In the winter of 1758, however, owing to a very serious illness, he resigned from the army and returned to Mount Vernon to recuperate.

During the long and tedious weeks of sickness and recovery, Washington doubtless had time to think over, to clarify in his mind, and to pass judgment on the events in which he had shared during the past six or seven years. From boyhood that was his habit. He must know the meaning of things. An event might be as fruitless as a shooting star unless he could trace the relations which tied it to what came before and after. Hence his deliberation which gave to his opinions the solidity of wisdom. Audacious he might be in battle, but perhaps what seems to us audacity seemed to him at the moment a higher prudence. If there were crises when the odds looked ten to one against him, he would take the chance. He knew the incalculable value of courage. His experiences with the British regulars and their officers left a deep impression on him and colored his own decisions in his campaigns against the British during the Revolutionary War. To genius nothing comes amiss, and by genius nothing is forgotten. So we find that all that Washington saw and learned during his years of youth — his apprenticeship as surveyor, his vicissitudes as pioneer, tasks as Indian fighter and as companion of the defeated Braddock — all contributed to fit him for the supreme work for which Fate had created him and the ages had waited.

CHAPTER II

MARRIAGE. THE LIFE OF A PLANTER

WAR is like the wind, nobody can tell into whose garden it may blow desolation. The French and Indian War, generally called now the Seven Years' War, beginning as a mere border altercation between the British and French backwoodsmen on the banks of the upper Ohio River, grew into a struggle which, by the year 1758, when Washington retired from his command of the Virginia Forces, spread over the world. A new statesman, one of the ablest ever born in England, came to control the English Government. William Pitt, soon created Earl of Chatham, saw that the British Empire had reached a crisis in its development. Incompetence, inertia, had blurred its prestige, and the little victories which France, its chief enemy, had been winning against it piecemeal, were coming to be regarded as signs that the grandeur of Britain was passing. Pitt saw the gloomy situation, and the still gloomier future which it seemed to prophesy, but he saw also the remedy. Within a few months, under his direction, English troops were in every part of the world, and English ships of war were sailing every ocean, to recover the slipping elements and to solidify the British Empire. Just as Pitt was taking up his residence at Downing Street, Robert Clive was winning the Battle of Plassey in India, which brought to England territory of untold wealth. Two years later James Wolfe, defeating the French commander, Montcalm, on the Plains of Abraham, added not only Quebec, but all Canada, to the British Crown, and ended French rivalry north of the Great Lakes. Victories like these, seemingly so casual, really as final and as unrevisable as Fate, might well cause Englishmen to suspect that Destiny itself worked with them, and that an Englishman could be trusted to endure through any difficulties to a triumphant conclusion.

Beaten at every point where they met the British, the French, even after they had secured an alliance with Spain, which proved of little worth, were glad to make peace. On February 10, 1763, they signed the Treaty of Paris, which confirmed to the British nearly all their victories and left England the dominant Power in both hemispheres. The result of the war produced a marked effect on the people of the British Colonies in North America. "At no period of time," says Chief Justice Marshall, in his "Life of Washington," "was the attachment of the colonists to the mother country more strong, or more general, than in 1763, when the definitive articles of the treaty which restored peace to Great Britain, France, and Spain, were signed." [1] But we who know the sequel perceive that the Seven Years' War not only strengthened the attachment between the Colonies and the Mother Country, but that it also made the Colonies aware of their common interests, and awakened among them mutual friendship, and in a very brief time their sense of unity prevailed over their temporary enthusiasm for England. George III, a monarch as headstrong as he was narrow, with insanity lurking in his mind, succeeded to the throne in 1760, and he seized the first opportunity to get rid of his masterful Minister, William Pitt. He replaced him with the Earl of Bute, a Scotchman, and a man of ingenious parts, but with the incurable Tory habit of insisting that it was still midnight long after the sun was shining in the forenoon of another day.

Before the Treaty was signed and the world had begun to spin in a new groove, which optimists thought would stretch on forever, an equally serious change had come to the private life of George Washington. To the surprise of his friends, who had begun to doubt whether he would ever get married, he found his life's companion and married her without delay.

[1] Marshall: *The Life of George Washington* (Philadelphia, 1805, 5 vols.), II, 68.

The notion seems to have been popular during his lifetime, and it certainly has continued to later days, that he was too bashful to feel easy in ladies' society. I find no evidence for this mistaken idea. Although little has been recorded of the intimacies of Washington's youth, there are indications of more than one "flame" and that he was not dull and stockish with the young women. As early as 1748, we hear of the Low-Land Beauty who had captivated him, and who is still to be identified. Even earlier, in his school days, he indulged in writing love verses. But we need not infer that they were inspired by living damsels or by the Muses.

"Oh ye Gods why should my poor resistless Heart
Stand to oppose thy might and power —

"In deluding sleepings let my eyelids close
That in an enraptured dream I may
In a rapt lulling sleep and gentle repose
Possess those joys denied by day." [1]

Cavour said that it was easier for him to make Italy than to write a poem: Washington, who was also an honest man, and fully aware of his limitations, would probably have admitted that he could make the American Republic more easily than a love song. But he was susceptible to feminine charms, and we hear of Betsy Fauntleroy, and of a "Mrs.

[1] Quoted by Wister, 39.

Meil," and on his return to Mount Vernon, after Braddock's defeat, he received the following round robin from some of the young ladies at Belvoir:

DEAR SIR, — After thanking Heaven for your safe return I must accuse you of great unkindness in refusing us the pleasure of seeing you this night. I do assure you nothing but our being satisfied that our company would be disagreeable should prevent us from trying if our legs would not carry us to Mount Vernon this night, but if you will not come to us tomorrow morning very early we shall be at Mount Vernon.

S[ALLY] FAIRFAX
ANN SPEARING
ELIZ'TH DENT

Apparently Washington's love affairs were known and talked about among his group. What promised to be the most serious of his experiences was with Mary Philipse, of New York, daughter of Frederick Philipse, one of the richest landowners in that Colony, and sister-in-law of Beverly Robinson, one of Washington's Virginian friends. Washington was going to Boston on a characteristic errand. One of the minor officers in the Regular British Army, which had accompanied Braddock to Virginia, refused to take orders from Washington, and officers of higher grade in Virginia Troops, declaring that their commissions were assigned only by Colonial officials, whereas he had his own from King George. This led, of course, to insubordination and frequent quarrels. To put a stop to the wrangling, Washington journeyed to Boston, to have Governor Shirley, the Commander-in-Chief of the King's Forces in the Colonies, give a decision upon it. The Governor ruled in favor of Washington, who then rode back to Virginia. But he spent a week in New York City in order to see his enchantress, Mary Philipse, and it is even whispered that he proposed to her and that she refused him. Two years afterwards she married Lieutenant-Colonel Roger Morris, and during the Revolution the Morris house was Washington's headquarters; the Morrises, who were Tories, having fled.

Persons have speculated why it was that so many of the young women whom Washington took a fancy to, chilled and drew back when it came to the question of marriage. One very clever writer thinks that perhaps his nose was inordinately large in his youth, and that that repelled them. I do not pretend to say. So far as I know, psychologists have not yet made a sufficiently exact study of the nose as a determining factor in matrimony, to warrant an opinion from persons who have made no special study of the subject. The plain fact was that by his twenty-fifth year, Washington was an unusually presentable young man, more than six feet tall, broad-shouldered, very strong, slender and athletic, carefully polite in his manners, a boon companion, though he talked little, a sound and deliberate thinker; moreover, the part he had taken in the war with the Indians and the French made him almost a popular hero, and gave him a preëminent place among the Virginians, both the young and the old, of that time. The possession of the estate of Mount Vernon, which he had inherited from his half-brother, Lawrence, assured to him more than a comfortable fortune, and yet gossip wondered why he was not married. Thackeray intimates that Washington was too evidently on the lookout for a rich wife, which, if true, may account for some of the alleged rebuffs. I do not believe this assertion, nor do I find evidence for it. Washington was always a very careful, farseeing person, and no doubt had a clear idea of what constitutes desirable qualifications in marriage, but I believe he would have married a poor girl out of the workhouse if he had really loved her. However, he was not put to that test.

One May day Washington rode off from Mount Vernon to carry despatches to Williamsburg. He stopped at William's Ferry for dinner with his friend Major Chamberlayne. At the table was Mrs. Daniel Parke Custis, who, under her maiden name of Martha Dandridge, was well known throughout that region for her beauty and sweet disposition. She was now a widow of twenty-six, with two small

children. Her late husband, Colonel Custis, her
elder by fifteen years, had left her a large estate
called White House, and a fortune which made her
one of the richest women in Virginia. From their
first introduction, Washington and she seemed to
be mutually attracted. He lingered throughout the
afternoon and evening with her and went on to
Williamsburg with his despatches the next morning.
Having finished his business at the Capitol, he returned to William's Ferry, where he again saw Mrs
Custis, pressed his suit upon her and was accepted
Characteristic was it that he should conclude the
matter so suddenly; but he had had marriage in his
intentions for many years.

During the summer Washington returned to his
military duties and led a troop to Fort Duquesne.
He found the fort partly demolished, and abandoned
by the French; he marched in and took it, and gave it
the name of Fort Pitt, in recognition of the great
statesman who had directed the revival of British
prestige. The fort, thus recovered to English possession, stood on the present site of Pittsburgh. I
quote the following brief letter from Washington to
Mrs. Custis, as it is almost the only note of his to her
during their engagement that has been preserved:

We have begun our March for the Ohio. A courier is
starting for Williamsburg, and I embrace the opportu-

By Gilbert Stuart

nity to send a few words to one whose life is now inseparable from mine. Since that happy hour when we made
our pledges to each other, my thoughts have been continually going to you as another Self. That an all powerful Providence may keep us both in safety is the prayer
of your ever faithful and affectionate friend.[1]

Late in that autumn Washington returned for good
from his Western fighting. On January 6, 1759 (Old
Style), his marriage to Mrs. Custis took place in St.
Peter's Church, near her home at the White House.
Judging from the fine writing which old historians and
new have devoted to describing it, Virginia had seen
few such elegant pageants as upon that occasion.
The grandees in official station and in social life were
all there. Francis Fauquier was, of course, gorgeous
in his Governor's robes but he could not outshine
the bridegroom, in blue and silver with scarlet trimmings, and gold buckles at his knees, with his imperial physique and carriage. The Reverend Peter
Mossum conducted the Episcopal service, after
which the bride drove back with a coach and six
to the White House, while Washington, with other
gentlemen, rode on horseback beside her acting as
escort.

The bridal couple spent two or three months at the
White House. The Custis estates were large and in
so much need of oversight that if Washington had

[1] P. L. Ford, *The True George Washington*, 93.

not appeared at this time, a bailiff, or manager, would have had to be hired for them. Henceforth Washington seems to have added the care of the White House to that of Mount Vernon, and the two involved a burden which occupied most of his time, for he had retired from the army. His fellow citizens, however, had elected him a member of the House of Burgesses, a position he held for many years; going to Williamsburg every season to attend the sessions of the Assembly. On his first entrance to take his seat, Mr. Robinson, the Speaker, welcomed him in Virginia's name, and praised him for his high achievements. This so embarrassed the modest young member that he was unable to reply, upon which Speaker Robinson said, "Sit down, Mr. Washington, your modesty is equal to your valor, and that surpasses the power of any language that I possess." In all his life, probably, Washington never heard praise more genuine or more deserved. He had just passed his twenty-seventh year. In the House of Burgesses he had the reputation of being the silent member. He never acquired the art of a debater. He was neither quick at rebuttal nor at repartee, but so surely did his character impress itself on every one that when he spoke the Assembly almost took it for granted that he had said the final word on the subject under discussion. How careful he was to observe the scope and effects of parliamentary speaking appears from a letter which he wrote many years later.

Agriculture has always been a particularly fine training-ground for statesmen. To persons who do not watch it closely, it may seem monotonous. In reality, while the sum of the conditions of one year tally closely with those of another, the daily changes and variations create a variety which must be constantly watched and provided for. A sudden freshet and unseasonable access of heat or cold, a scourge of hail, a drought, a murrain among the cattle, call for ingenuity and for resourcefulness; and for courage, a higher moral quality. Constant comradeship with Nature seems to beget placidity and quiet assurance. From using the great natural forces which bring to pass crops and the seasons, they seem to work in and through him also. The banker, the broker, even the merchant, lives in a series of whirlwinds, or seems to be pursuing a mirage or groping his way through a fog. The farmer, although he be not beyond the range of accident, deals more continually with causes which regularly produce certain effects. He knows a rainbow by sight and does not waste his time and money in chasing it.

No better idea of Washington's activity as a planter can be had than from his brief and terse journals as an agriculturist. He sets down day by day what he did and what his slaves and the free employees did on all parts of his estate. We see him as a regular and punctual man. He had a moral repugnance to idleness. He himself worked steadily and he chided the incompetent, the shirkers, and the lazy.

A short experience as landowner convinced him that slave labor was the least efficient of all. This conviction led him very early to believe in the emancipation of the slaves. I do not find that sentiment or abstract ideals moved him to favor emancipation, but his sense of fitness, his aversion to wastefulness and inefficiency made him disapprove of a system which rendered industry on a high plane impossible. Experience only confirmed these convictions of his, and in his will he ordered that many slaves should be freed after the death of Mrs. Washington. He was careful to apportion to his slaves the amount of food they needed in order to keep in health and to work the required stint. He employed a doctor to look after them in sickness. He provided clothing for them which he deemed sufficient. I do not gather that he ever regarded the black man as being essentially made of the same clay as the white man, the chief difference being the color of their skin. To Washington, the Slave System seemed bad, not so much because it represented a debased moral stand-

... economically and socially ...racter appears in his mak-...hich he recognized as most ...ement, in a few years, his ...became the model of that ...South.

...erstand Washington's life ...is diaries with their brief, ...rusque, entries from day to ...nvolved not only bringing the Mount Vernon estate to the highest point of prosperity by improving the productiveness of its various sections, but also by buying and annexing new pieces of land. To such a planter as he was, the ideal was to raise enough food to supply all the persons who lived or worked on the place, and this he succeeded in doing. His chief source of income, which provided him with ready money, was the tobacco crop, which proved to be of uncertain value. By Washington's time the Virginians had much diminished the amount and delicacy of the tobacco they raised by the careless methods they employed. They paid little attention to the rotation of crops, or to manuring, with the result that the soil was never properly replenished. In his earlier days Washing-

[1] See for instance in W. C. Ford's edition of *The Writings of George Washington*, II, 140–69. Diary for 1760, 230–56. Diary for 1768.

ton shipped his year's product to an agent in Glasgow or in London, who sold it at the market price and sent him the proceeds. The process of transportation was sometimes precarious; a leaky ship might let in enough sea water to damage the tobacco, and there was always the risk of loss by shipwreck or other accident. Washington sent out to his brokers a list of things which he desired to pay for out of the proceeds of the sale, to be sent to him. These lists are most interesting, as they show us the sort of household utensils and furniture, the necessaries and the luxuries, and the apparel used in a mansion like Mount Vernon. We find that he even took care to order a fashionably dressed doll for little Martha Custis to play with.

The care and education of little Martha and her brother, John Parke Custis, Washington undertook with characteristic thoroughness and solicitude. He had an instinct for training growing creatures. He liked to experiment in breeding horses and cattle and the farmyard animals. He watched the growth of his plantations of trees, and he was all the more interested in studying the development of mental and moral capacities in the little children.

In due time a tutor was engaged, and besides the lessons they learned in their schoolbooks, they were taught both music and dancing. Little Patsy suffered from epilepsy, and after the prescriptions of the regular doctors had done no good, her parents turned to a quack named Evans, who placed on the child's finger an iron ring supposed to have miraculous virtues, but it brought her no relief, and very suddenly little Martha Custis died. Washington himself felt the loss of his unfortunate stepdaughter, but he was unflagging in trying to console the mother, heartbroken at the death of the child.

Jack Custis was given in charge of the Reverend Jonathan Boucher, an Anglican clergyman, apparently well-meaning, who agreed with Washington's general view that the boy's training "should make him fit for more useful purposes than horse-racing." In spite of Washington's carefully reasoned plans, the youth of the young man prevailed over the reason of his stepfather. Jack found dogs, horses, and guns, and consideration of dress more interesting and more important than his stepfather's theories of education. Washington wrote to Parson Boucher, the teacher:

Had he begun, or rather pursued his study of the Greek language, I should have thought it no bad acquisition; . . . To be acquainted with the French Tongue is become a part of polite education; and to a man who has the prospect of mixing in a large circle, absolutely necessary. Without arithmetic, the common affairs of life are not to be managed with success. The study of Ge-

ometry, and the mathematics (with due regard to the
limits of it) is equally advantageous. The principles of
Philosophy, Moral, Natural, etc. I should think a very
desirable knowledge for a gentleman.[1]

There was nothing abstract in young Jack Custis's practical response to his stepfather's reasoning;
he fell in love with Miss Nelly Calvert and asked her
to marry him. Washington was forced to plead with
the young lady that the youth was too young for
marriage by several years, and that he must finish
his education. Apparently she acquiesced without
making a scene. She accepted a postponement of the
engagement, and Custis was enrolled among the
students of King's College (subsequently Columbia)
in New York City. Even then, his passion for an education did not develop as his parents hoped. He
left the college in the course of a few months.
Throughout John Custis's perversities, and as long
as he lived, Washington's kindness and real affection never wavered. Although he had now taught
himself to practice complete self-control, he could
treat with consideration the young who had it not.

By nature Washington was a man of business. He
wished to see things grow, not so much for the actual
increase in value which that indicated, as because
increase seemed to be a proof of proper methods.

[1] W. C. Ford, *George Washington* (1900), I, 136–37.

Not content, therefore, with rounding out his holdings at Mount Vernon and Mrs. Washington's estate at the White House, he sought investment in the unsettled lands on the Ohio and in Florida, and on the Mississippi. It proved to be a long time before the advance of settlement in the latter regions made his investments worth much, and during the decade after his marriage in 1759, we must think of him as a man of great energy and calm judgment who was bent not only on making Mount Vernon a model country place on the outside, but a civilized home within. In its furnishings and appointments it did not fall behind the manors of the Virginia men of fashion and of wealth in that part of the country. Before Washington left the army, he recognized that his education had been irregular and inadequate, and he set himself to make good his defects by studying and reading for himself. There were no public libraries, but some of the gentlemen made collections of books. They learned of new publications in England from journals which were few in number and incomplete. Doubtless advertising went by word of mouth. The lists of things desired which Washington sent out to his agents, Robert Cary and Company, once a year or oftener, usually contained the titles of many books, chiefly on architecture, and he was especially intent on keeping up with new

methods and experiments in farming. Thus, among
the orders in May, 1759, among a request for "Des-
ert Glasses and Stand for Sweetmeats Jellies, etc.;
50 lbs. Spirma Citi Candles; stockings etc.," he
asks for "the newest and most approved Treatise of
Agriculture — besides this, send me a Small piece
in Octavo — called a New System of Agriculture,
or a Speedy Way to Grow Rich; Longley's Book of
Gardening; Gibson upon Horses, the latest Edition
in Quarto." This same invoice contains directions
for "the Busts" — one of Alexander the Great, another of Charles XII, of Sweden, and a fourth of the
King of Prussia (Frederick the Great); also of Prince
Eugene and the Duke of Marlborough, but "somewhat smaller." Do these celebrities represent Washington's heroes in 1759?

As time went on, his commissions for books were
less restricted to agriculture, and comprised also
works on history, biography, and government.

But although incessant activity devoted to various
kinds of work was a characteristic of Washington's
life at Mount Vernon, his attention to social duties
and pleasures was hardly less important. He aimed
to be a country gentleman of influence, and he knew
that he could achieve this only by doing his share of
the bountiful hospitality which was expected of such
a personage. Virginia at that time possessed no

large cities or towns with hotels. When the gentry travelled, they put up overnight at the houses of other gentry, and thus, in spite of very restricted means of transportation, the inhabitants of one part of the country exchanged ideas with those of another. In this way also the members of the upper class circulated among themselves and acquired a solidarity which otherwise would hardly have been possible. We are told that Mount Vernon was always full of guests; some of these being casual strangers travelling through, and others being invited friends and acquaintances on a visit. There were frequent balls and parties when neighbors from far and near joined in some entertainment at the great mansion. There were the hunt balls which Washington himself particularly enjoyed, hunting being his favorite sport. Fairfax County, where Mount Vernon lay, and its neighboring counties, Fauquier and Prince William, abounded in foxes, and the land was not too difficult for the hunters, who copied as far as possible the dress and customs of the foxhunters in England. Possibly there might be a meeting at Mount Vernon of the local politicians. At least once a year Washington and his wife — "Lady," as the somewhat florid Virginians called her — went off to Williamsburg to attend the session of the House of Burgesses. Washington seldom missed going to the horse-races, one of the chief functions of the year, not only for jockeys and sporting men, but for the fashionable world of the aristocracy. Thanks to his carefulness and honesty in keeping his accounts, we have his own record of the amounts he spent at cards — never large amounts, nor indicative of the gamester's passion.

Thus Washington passed the first ten years of his married life. A stranger meeting him at that time might have little suspected that here was the future founder of a nation, one who would prove himself the greatest of Americans, if not the greatest of men. But if you had spent a day with Washington, and watched him at work, or listened to his few but decisive words, or seen his benign but forcible smile, you would have said to yourself — "This man is equal to any fate that destiny may allot to him."

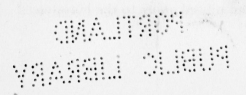

CHAPTER III

THE FIRST GUN

MEANWHILE the course of events was leading toward a new and unexpected goal. Chief Justice Marshall said, as I have quoted, that 1763, the end of the French-Indian War, marked the greatest friendship and harmony between the Colonies and England. The reason is plain. In their incessant struggles with the French and the Indians, the Colonists had discovered a real champion and protector. That protector, England, had found that she must really protect the Colonies unless she was willing to see them fall into the hands of her rival, France. Putting forth her strength, she crushed France in America, and remained virtually in control not only of the Colonies and territory from the Atlantic to the Mississippi, but also of British America. In these respects the Colonies and the Mother Country seemed destined to be bound more closely together; but the very spirit by which Britain had conquered France in America, and France in India, and had made England paramount throughout the world, prevented the further fusion, moral, social, and political, of the Colonies with the Mother Country.

That spirit was the Imperial Spirit, which Plassey and Quebec had called to life. The narrow Hanoverian King, who now ruled England, could not himself have devised the British Empire, but when the Empire crystallized, George III rightly surmised that, however it had come about, it meant a large increase in power for him. The Colonies and Dependencies were to be governed like conquered provinces. Evidently, the Hindus of Bengal could hardly be treated in the same fashion as were the Colonists of Massachusetts or Virginia. The Bengalese knew that there was no bond of language or of race between them and their conquerors, whereas American Colonists knew that they and the British sprang from the same race and spoke the same language. One of the first realizations that came to the British Imperialists was that the ownership of the conquered people or state warranted the conquerors in enriching themselves from the conquered. But while this might do very well in India, and be accepted there as a matter of course, it would be most ill-judged in the American Colonies, for the Colonists were not a foreign nor a conquered people. They originally held grants of land from the British Crown, but they had worked that land themselves and settled the wilderness by their own efforts, and had a right to whatever they might earn.

The Tory ideals, which took possession of the British Government when Lord Bute succeeded to William Pitt in power, were soon applied to England's relations to the American Colonies. The Seven Years' War left England heavily in debt. She needed larger revenues, and being now swayed by Imperialism, she easily found reasons for taxing the Colonies. In 1765 she passed the Stamp Act which caused so much bad feeling that in less than a year she decided to repeal it, but new duties on paper, glass, tea, and other commodities were imposed instead. In the North, Massachusetts took the lead in opposing what the Colonists regarded as the unconstitutional acts of the Crown. The patriotic lawyer of Boston, James Otis, shook the Colony with his eloquence against the illegal encroachments and actual tyranny of the English. Other popular orators of equal eminence, John and Samuel Adams and Josiah Quincy, fanned the flames of discontent. Even the most radical did not yet whisper the terrible word Revolution, or suggest that they aspired to independence. They simply demanded their "rights" which the arrogant and testy British Tories had shattered and were withholding from them. At the outset rebels seldom admit that their rebellion aims at new acquisitions, but only at the recovery of the old.

Next to Massachusetts, Virginia was the most

vigorous of the Colonies in protesting against British usurpation of power, which would deprive them of their liberty. Although Virginia had no capital city like Boston, in which the chief political leaders might gather and discuss and plan, and mobs might assemble and equip with physical force the impulses of popular indignation, the Old Dominion had means, just as the Highland clans or the Arab tribes had, of keeping in touch with each other. Patrick Henry, a young Virginia lawyer of sturdy Scotch descent, by his flaming eloquence was easily first among the spokesmen of the rights of the Colonists in Virginia. In the "Parsons Cause," a lawsuit which might have passed quickly into oblivion had he not seen the vital implications concerned in it, he denied the right of the King to veto an act of the Virginia Assembly, which had been passed for the good of the people of Virginia. In the course of the trial he declared, "Government was a conditional compact between the King, stipulating protection on the one hand, and the people, stipulating obedience and support on the other," and he asserted that a violation of these covenants by either party discharged the other party from its obligations. Doctrines as outspoken as these uttered in court, whether right or wrong, indicated that the attorney who uttered them, and the judge who listened, and the audience who applauded, were not blind worshippers of the illegal rapacity of the Crown.

Patrick Henry was the most spectacular of the early champions of the Colonists in Virginia, but many others of them agreed with him. Among these the weightiest was the silent George Washington. He said little, but his opinions passed from mouth to mouth, and convinced many. In 1765 he wrote to Francis Dandridge, an uncle of Mrs. Washington:

The Stamp Act imposed on the colonies by the Parliament of Great Britain, engrosses the conversation of the speculative part of the colonists, who look upon this unconstitutional method of taxation, as a direful attack upon their liberties, and loudly exclaim against the violation. What may be the result of this, and of some other (I think I may add) ill-judged measures, I will not undertake to determine; but this I may venture to affirm, that the advantage accruing to the mother country will fall greatly short of the expectations of the ministry; for certain it is, that an whole substance does already in a manner flow to Great Britain, and that whatsoever contributes to lessen our importations must be hurtful to their manufacturers. And the eyes of our people, already beginning to open, will perceive, that many luxuries, which we lavish our substance in Great Britain for, can well be dispensed with, whilst the necessaries of life are (mostly) to be had within ourselves. This, consequently, will introduce frugality, and be a necessary stimulation to industry. If Great Britain, therefore, loads her manufacturies with heavy taxes, will it not facilitate these measures? They will not compel us, I think, to give our money for their exports, whether we will or not; and certain I am, none of their traders will part from them without a valuable consideration. Where then, is the utility of the restrictions?

As to the Stamp Act, taken in a single view, one and the first bad consequence attending it, I take to be this, our courts of judicature must inevitably be shut up; for it is impossible, (or next of kin to it), under our present circumstances, that the act of Parliament can be complied with, were we ever so willing to enforce the execution; for, not to say, which alone would be sufficient, that we have not money to pay the stamps, there are many other cogent reasons, to prevent it; and if a stop be put to our judicial proceedings, I fancy the merchants of Great Britain, trading to the colonies, will not be among the last to wish for a repeal of it.[1]

This passage would suffice, were there not many similar which might be quoted, to prove that Washington was from the start a loyal American. A legend which circulated during his lifetime, and must have been fabricated by his enemies, for I find no evidence to support it either in his letters or in other trustworthy testimony, insinuated that he was British at heart and threw his lot in with the Colonists only when war could not be averted. In 1770 the merchants of Philadelphia drew up an agreement in which they pledged themselves to practise non-importation of British goods sent to America. Washington's wise neighbor and friend, George Mason, drafted a plan of association of similar purport to be

[1] Ford, II, 209–10.

laid before the Virginia Burgesses. But Lord Bote-
tourt, the new Royal Governor, deemed some of
these resolutions dangerous to the prerogative of the
King, and dissolved the Assembly. The Burgesses,
however, met at Anthony Hay's house and adopted
Mason's Association. Washington, who was one of
the signers of the Association, wrote to his agents in
London: "I am fully determined to adhere religiously
to it."

Five years had now elapsed since the British Tories attempted to fix on the Colonies the Stamp Act,
and although they had withdrawn that hateful law,
the relations between the Mother Country and the
Colonists had not improved. Far from it. The
English issued a series of irritating provisions which
convinced the Colonists that the Government had
no real desire to be friendly, and that, on the contrary, it intended to make no distinction between
them and the other conquered provinces of the
Crown. Then and always, the English forgot that
the Colonists were men of their own stock, equally
stubborn in their devotion to principles, and probably more accessible to scruples of conscience. So
they were not likely to be frightened into subjection.
The governing class in England was in a state of
mind which has darkened its judgment more than
once; the state of mind which, when it encounters an

obstacle to its plans, regards that obstacle as an enemy, and remarks in language brutally frank, though not wholly elegant: "We will lick him first and then decide who is right." In 1770 King George III, who fretted at all seasons at the slowness with which he was able to break down the ascendency of the Whigs, manipulated the Government so as to make Lord North Prime Minister. Lord North was a servant, one might say a lackey, after the King's own heart. He abandoned lifelong traditions, principles, fleeting whims, prejudices even, in order to keep up with the King's wish of the moment. After Lord North became Prime Minister, the likelihood of a peaceful settlement between the crown and the Colonies lessened. He ran ahead of the King in his desire to serve the King's wishes, and George III, by this time, was wrought up by the persistent tenacity of the Whigs — he wished them dead, but they would not die — and he was angered by the insolence of the Colonists who showed that they would not shrink from forcibly resisting the King's command. On both sides of the Atlantic a vehement and most enlightening debate over constitutional and legal fundamentals still went on. Although the King had packed Parliament, not all the oratory poured out at Westminster favored the King. On the contrary, the three chief masters of British eloquence at that time, and in all time — Edmund Burke, William Pitt, and Charles James Fox — spoke on the side of the Colonists. Reading the magnificent arguments of Burke to-day, we ask ourselves how any group in Parliament could have withstood them. But there comes a moment in every vital discussion when arguments and logic fail to convince. Passions deeper than logic controlled motives and actions. The Colonists contended that in proclaiming "no taxation without representation," they were appealing to a principle of Anglo-Saxon liberty inherent in their race. When King George, or any one else, denied this principle, he denied an essential without which Anglo-Saxon polity could not survive, but neither King George nor Lord North accepted the premises. If they had condescended to reply at all, they might have sung the hymn of their successors a hundred years later:

> "We don't want to fight,
>   But by jingo! if we do,
>   We've got the men, we've got the ships,
>   We've got the money too."

Meanwhile, the Virginia Planter watched the course of events, pursued his daily business regularly, attended the House of Burgesses when it was in session, said little, but thought much. He did not break out into invective or patriotic appeals. No doubt many of his acquaintances thought him luke-warm in spirit and non-committal; but persons who knew him well knew what his decision must be. As early as April 5, 1769, he wrote his friend, George Mason:

At a time, when our lordly masters in Great Britain will be satisfied with nothing less than the deprivation of American freedom, it seems highly necessary that something should be done to avert the stroke, and main-tain the liberty, which we have derived from our ances-tors. But the manner of doing it, to answer the purpose effectually, is the point in question.

That no man should scruple, or hesitate a moment, to use a—ms in defence of so valuable a blessing, on which all the good and evil of life depends, is clearly my opinion. Yet a—ms, I would beg leave to add, should be the last resource, the dernier resort. Addresses to the throne, and remonstrances to Parliament, we have already, it is said, proved the inefficiency of. How far, then, their attention to our rights and privileges is to be awakened or alarmed, by starving their trade and manufacturers, remains to be tried.[1]

Thus wrote the Silent Member six years before the outbreak of hostilities, and he did not then dis-play any doubt either of his patriotism, or of the course which every patriot must take. To his inti-mates he spoke with point-blank candor. Years later, George Mason wrote to him:

I never forgot your declaration, when I had last the pleasure of being at your house in 1768, that you were

[1] Ford, II, 263–64.

ready to take your musket upon your shoulder whenever your country called upon you.

Some writers point out that Washington excelled rather as a critic of concrete plans than of constitutional and legal aspects. Perhaps this is true. Assuredly he had no formal legal training. There were many other men in Massachusetts, in Virginia, and in some of the other Colonies, who could and did analyze minutely the Colonists' protest against taxation without representation, and the British rebuttal thereof; but Washington's strength lay in his primal wisdom, the wisdom which is based not on conventions, even though they be laws and constitutions, but on a knowledge of the ways in which men will react toward each other in their primitive, natural relations. In this respect he was one of the wisest among the statesmen.

He does not seem to have joined in such clandestine methods as those of the Committees of Correspondence, which Samuel Adams and some of the most radical patriots in the Bay State had organized, but he said in the Virginia Convention, in 1774: "I will raise one thousand men, subsist them at my own expense and march myself at their head for the relief of Boston." [1] The ardor of Washington's offer matched the increasing anger of the Colonists. Lord

[1] *John Adams's Diary*, August 31, 1774, quoting Lynch.

North, abetted by the British Parliament, had continued to exasperate them by passing new bills which could have produced under the best circumstances only a comparatively small revenue. One of these imposed a tax on tea. The Colonists not only refused to buy it, but to have it landed. In Boston a large crowd gathered and listened to much fiery speech-making. Suddenly, a body of fifty men disguised as Mohawk Indians rushed down to the wharves, rowed out to the three vessels in which a large consignment of tea had been sent across the ocean, hoisted it out of the holds to the decks and scattered the contents of three hundred and forty chests in Boston Harbor.

The Boston Tea Party was as sensational as if it had sprung from the brain of a Paris Jacobin in the French Revolution. It created excitement among the American Colonists from Portsmouth to Charleston. Six more of the Colonies enrolled Committees of Correspondence, Pennsylvania alone refusing to join. In every quarter American patriots felt exalted. In England the reverse effects were signalized with equal vehemence. The Mock Indians were denounced as incendiaries, and the town meetings were condemned as "nurseries of sedition." Parliament passed four penal laws, the first of which punished Boston by transferring its port to Salem and closing its harbor. The second law suspended the charter of the Province and added several new and tyrannical powers to the British Governor and to Crown officials.

On September 5, 1774, the first Continental Congress met in Philadelphia. Except Georgia, every Colony sent delegates to it. The election of those delegates was in several cases irregular, because the body which chose them was not the Legislature but some temporary body of the patriots. Nevertheless, the Congress numbered some of the men who were actually and have remained in history, the great engineers of the American Revolution. Samuel Adams and John Adams went from Massachusetts; John Jay and Robert R. Livingston from New York; Roger Sherman and Oliver Ellsworth from Connecticut; Alexander Hamilton and Thomas McKean from Pennsylvania; George Washington, Patrick Henry, and Thomas Jefferson, and the Pendletons and Randolphs from Virginia; and the Rutledges and Pinckneys from South Carolina. Although the Congress was made up of these men and of others like them, the petitions adopted by it and the work done, not to mention the freshets of oratory, were astonishingly mild. Probably many of the delegates would have preferred to use fiery tongues. Samuel Adams, for instance, though "prematurely gray, palsied in hand, and trembling in voice," must have had dif-

ficulty in restraining himself. He wrote as viciously
as he spoke. "Damn that Adams," said one of his
enemies. "Every dip of his pen stings like a horned
snake." Patrick Henry, being asked when he returned home, "Who is the greatest man in Congress,"
replied: "If you speak of eloquence, Mr. Rutledge
of South Carolina is by far the greatest orator; but
if you speak of solid information and sound judgment, Colonel Washington is unquestionably the
greatest man on that floor." The rumor had it that
Washington said, he wished to God the Liberties
of America were to be determined by a single Combat between himself and George. One other saying
of his at this time is worth reporting, although it
cannot be satisfactorily verified. "*More blood will
be spilled on this occasion*, if the ministry are determined to push matters to extremity, *than history has
ever yet furnished instances of* in the annals of North
America." The language and tone of the "Summary
View" — a pamphlet which Thomas Jefferson had
issued shortly before — probably chimed with the
emotions of most of the delegates. They adopted
(October 14, 1774) the "Declaration of Rights,"
which may not have seemed belligerent enough for
the Radicals, but really leaves little unsaid. A week
later Congress agreed to an "Association," an in-
strument for regulating, by preventing, trade with

COLONEL GEORGE WASHINGTON

By Charles Willson Peale, 1772

the English. Having provided for the assembling of a second Congress, the first adjourned.

As a symbol, the First Congress has an integral importance in the growth of American Independence. It marked the first time that the American Colonies had acted together for their collective interests. It served notice on King George and Lord North that it repudiated the claims of the British Parliament to govern the Colonies. It implied that it would repel by force every attempt of the British to exercise an authority which the Colonists refused to recognize. In a very real sense the Congress thus delivered an ultimatum. The winter of 1774/5 saw preparations being pushed on both sides. General Thomas Gage, the British Commander-in-Chief stationed at Boston, had also thrust upon him the civil government of that town. He had some five thousand British troops in Boston, and several men-of-war in the harbor. There were no overt acts, but the speed with which, on more than one occasion, large bodies of Colonial farmers assembled and went swinging through the country to rescue some place, which it was falsely reported the British were attacking, showed the nervous tension under which the Americans were living. As the enthusiasm of the Patriots increased, that of the Loyalists increased also. Among the latter were many of the rich and aristocratic inhabitants, and, of course, most of the office-holders. Until the actual outbreak of hostilities they upheld the King's cause with more chivalry than discretion, and then they migrated to Nova Scotia and to England, and bore the penalty of confiscation and the corroding distress of exile. In England during this winter, Pitt and Burke had defended the Colonies and the Whig minority had supported them. Even Lord North used conciliatory suggestions, but with him conciliation meant that the Colonies should withdraw all their offensive demands and kneel before the Crown in penitent humiliation before a new understanding could be thought of.

Meanwhile Colonel Washington was in Virginia running his plantations to the best of his ability and with his mind made up. He wrote to his friend Bryan Fairfax (July 20, 1774):

As I see nothing, on the one hand, to induce a belief that the Parliament would embrace a favorable opportunity of repealing acts, which they go on with great rapidity to pass, and in order to enforce their tyrannical system; and on the other, I observe, or think I observe, that government is pursuing a regular plan at the expense of law and justice to overthrow our constitutional rights and liberties, how can I expect any redress from a measure, which has been ineffectually tried already? For, Sir, what is it we are contending against? Is it against paying the duty of three pence per pound on tea because burthensome? No, it is the right only, we have all along disputed, and to this end we have already petitioned his Majesty in as humble and dutiful manner as subjects could do.[1] . . .

And has not General Gage's conduct since his arrival, (in stopping the address of his Council, and publishing a proclamation more becoming a Turkish bashaw, than an English governor, declaring it treason to associate in any manner by which the commerce of Great Britain is to be affected) exhibited an unexampled testimony of the most despotic system of tyranny, that ever was practised in a free government? In short, what further proofs are wanted to satisfy one of the designs of the ministry, than their own acts, which are uniform and plainly tending to the same point, nay, if I mistake not, avowedly to fix the right of taxation? What hope then from petitioning, when they tell us, that now or never is the time to fix the matter? Shall we after this, whine and cry for relief, when we have already tried it in vain? Or shall we supinely sit and see one province after another fall a prey to despotism? [2]

In the early autumn Washington wrote to Captain Robert MacKenzie, who was serving in the Regular British Army with Gage at Boston:

I think I can announce it as a fact, that it is not the wish or intent of that government, (Massachusetts) or any other upon this continent, separately or collectively, to set up for independence; but this you may at the same time rely on, that none of them will ever submit to the loss of these valuable rights and privileges, which are essential to the happiness of every free state, and without which, life, liberty, and property are rendered totally insecure.[3]

In the following spring the battles of Lexington

---

[1] Ford, II, 421–22.　　[2] *Ibid.*, 423–24.　　[3] *Ibid.*, 443.

and Concord, on April 19th, began the war of the American Revolution. A few weeks later, a Second Continental Congress met in Philadelphia. The delegates to it, understanding that they must prepare for war, proceeded to elect a Commander-in-Chief. There was some jealousy between the men of Virginia and those of Massachusetts. The former seemed to think that the latter assumed the first position, and indeed, most of the angry gestures had been made in Boston, and Boston had been the special object of British punishment. Still, with what may seem unexpected self-effacement, they did not press strongly for the choice of a Massachusetts man as Commander-in-Chief. On June 15, 1775, Congress having resolved "that a general be appointed to command all the continental forces raised or to be raised for the defence of American liberty," proceeded to a choice, and the ballots being taken, George Washington, Esq., was unanimously elected. On the next day the President of the Congress, Mr. John Hancock, formally announced the election to Colonel Washington, who replied:

Mr. President, though I am truly sensible of the high honor done me in this appointment, yet I feel great distress from a consciousness that my abilities and military experience may not be equal to the extensive and important trust. However, as the Congress desire it, I will enter upon the momentous duty and exert every

power I possess in the service and for the support of the
glorious cause. I beg they will accept my most cordial
thanks for this distinguished testimony of their approbation. But lest some unlucky event should happen
unfavorable to my reputation, I beg it may be remembered by every gentleman in the room, that I this day
declare with the utmost sincerity I do not think myself equal to the command I am honored with.

As to pay, Sir, I beg leave to assure the Congress, that
as no pecuniary consideration could have tempted me
to accept this arduous employment at the expense of
my domestic ease and happiness, I do not wish to make
any profit from it. I will keep an exact account of my
expenses. Those I doubt not they will discharge, and
that is all I desire.[1]

Accompanied by Lee and Schuyler and a brilliant
escort, he set forth on June 21st for Boston. Before
they had gone twenty miles a messenger bringing
news of the Battle of Bunker Hill crossed them.
"Did the Militia fight?" Washington asked. On
being told that they did, he said: "Then the liberties of the country are safe." Then he pushed on,
stopping long enough in New York to appoint General Schuyler military commander of that Colony,
and so through Connecticut to the old Bay State.
There, at Cambridge, he found the crowd awaiting
him and some of the Colonial troops. On the edge
of the Common, under a large elm tree broad of
spread, he took command of the first American
army. It was the second of July, 1775.

[1] Ford, II, 477–78–79, 480–81.

CHAPTER IV

BOSTON FREED

THUS began what seems to us now an impossible war. Although it had been brooding for ten years, since the Stamp Act, which showed that the ties of blood and of tradition meant nothing to the British Tories, now that it had come, the Colonists may well have asked themselves what it meant. Probably, if the Colonists had taken a poll on that fine July morning in 1775, not one in five of them would have admitted that he was going to war to secure Independence, but all would have protested that they would die if need be to recover their freedom, the old British freedom, which came down to them from Runnymede and should not be wrested from them.

A British Tory, at the same time, might have replied: "We fight, we cannot do less, in order to discipline and punish these wretches who assume to deny the jurisdiction of the British Crown and to rebel against the authority of the British Parliament." A few years before, an English general had boasted that with an army of five thousand troops he would undertake a march from Canada, through the Colonies, straight to the Gulf of Mexico. And Colonel

George Washington, who had seen something of the quality of the British regulars, remarked that with a thousand seasoned Virginians he would engage to block the five thousand wherever he met them. The test was now to be made.

The first thing that strikes us is the great extent of the field of war. From the farthest settlements in the northeast, in what is now Maine, to the border villages in Georgia was about fifteen hundred miles; but mere distance did not represent the difficulty of the journey. Between Boston and Baltimore ran a carriage road, not always kept in good repair. Most of the other stretches had to be traversed on horseback. The country along the seaboard was generally well supplied with food, but the supply was nowhere near large enough to furnish regular permanent subsistence for an army. A lack of munitions seriously threatened the Colonists' ability to fight at all, but the discovery of lead in Virginia made good this deficiency until the year 1781, when the lead mine was exhausted.

More important than material concerns, however, was the diversity in origin and customs among the Colonists themselves. The total population numbered in 1775 nearly two and one half million souls. Of these, the slaves formed about 500,000. The three largest Colonies, Virginia, Massachusetts, and

Pennsylvania contained 900,000 inhabitants, of which a little more than one half were slaves. Pennsylvania, the third Colony, had a total of 300,000, mostly white, while South Carolina had 200,000, of whom only 65,000 were white. Connecticut, on the other hand, had 200,000 with scarcely any blacks. The result was a very mottled population. The New Englanders had already begun to practise manufacturing, and they continued to raise under normal conditions sufficient food for their subsistence. South of the Mason and Dixon line, however, slave labor prevailed and the three great staples — tobacco, cotton, and rice — were the principal crops. Where these did not grow, the natives got along as best they could on scanty common crops, and by raising a few sheep and hogs. As the war proceeded, it taught with more and more force the inherent wastefulness of slave labor in the South. It was inefficient, costly, and unreliable.

The Battle of Bunker Hill was at once hailed as a Patriot victory, but the rejoicing was premature, for the Americans had been forced to retreat, giving up the position they had bravely defended. Nevertheless, the opinion prevailed that they had won a real victory by withstanding through many hours of a bloody fight some of the best of the British regiments in North America. A fortnight later, when Wash-

ington took command of the American army at
Cambridge, he was faced with the great task of
organizing it and of forming a plan of campaign.
The Congress had taken over the charge of the army
at Boston, and the events had so shaped themselves
that the first thing for Washington to do was to
drive out the British troops. To accomplish this he
planned to seal up all the entrances into the town by
land so that food could not be smuggled in. The
British had a considerable fleet in Boston Harbor,
and they had to rely upon it to bring provisions and
to keep in touch with the world outside.

Washington had his headquarters at the Craigie
House in Cambridge, some half a mile from Harvard
Square and the College. He was now forty-three
years old, a man of commanding presence, six feet
three inches tall, broad-shouldered but slender,
without any signs of the stoutness of middle age.
His hands and feet were large. His head was somewhat small. The blue-gray eyes, set rather far
apart, looked out from heavy eyebrows with an expression of attentiveness. The most marked feature
was the nose, which was fairly large and straight
and vigorous. The mouth shut firmly, as it usually
does where decision is the dominant trait. The lips
were flat. His color was pale but healthy, and rarely
flushed, even under great provocation.

All that had gone before seemed to be strangely blended in his appearance. The surveyor lad; the Indian fighter and officer; the planter; the foxhunter; the Burgess; you could detect them all. But underlying them all was the permanent Washington, deferent, plain of speech, direct, yet slow in forming or expressing an opinion. Most men, after they had been with him awhile, felt a sense of his majesty grow upon them, a sense that he was made of common flesh like them, but of something uncommon besides, something very high and very precious.

Washington found that he had sixteen thousand troops under his command near Boston. Of these two thirds came from Massachusetts, and Connecticut halved the rest. During July Congress added three thousand men from Pennsylvania, Maryland, and Virginia. They lacked everything. In order to give them some uniformity in dress, Washington suggested hunting-shirts, which he said "would have a happier tendency to unite the men and abolish those Provincial Distinctions which lead to jealousy and dissatisfaction." Among higher officers, jealousy, which they made no attempt to dissemble or to disguise, was common. Two of the highest posts went to Englishmen who proved themselves not only technically unfit, but suspiciously near disloyalty. One of these was Charles Lee, who thought the major-generalship to which Congress appointed him beneath his notice; the other was also an Englishman, Horatio Gates, Adjutant-General. A third, Thomas, when about to retire in pique, received from Washington the following rebuke:

In the usual contests of empire and ambition, the conscience of a soldier has so little share, that he may very properly insist upon his claims of rank, and extend his pretensions even to punctilio; — but in such a cause as this, when the object is neither glory nor extent of territory, but a defense of all that is dear and valuable in private and public life, surely every post ought to be deemed honorable in which a man can serve his country.[1]

Besides the complaints which reached Washington from all sides, he had also to listen to the advice of military amateurs. Some of these had never been in a battle and knew nothing about warfare except from reading, but they were not on this account the most taciturn. Many urged strongly that an expedition be sent against Canada, a design which Washington opposed. His wisdom was justified when Richard Montgomery, with about fifteen hundred men, took Montreal — November 12, 1775 — and after waiting several weeks formed a junction with Benedict Arnold near Quebec, which they attacked in a blinding snowstorm, December 31, 1775.

[1] Ford, *George Washington*, I, 175.

Arnold had marched up the Kennebec River and through the Maine wilderness with fifteen hundred men, which were reduced to five hundred before they came into action with Montgomery's much dwindled force. The commander of Quebec repulsed them and sent them flying southward as fast as the rigors of the winter and the difficulties of the wilderness permitted.

By the end of July, meanwhile, Washington had brought something like order into the undisciplined and untrained masses who formed his army, but now another lack threatened him: a lack of gunpowder. The cartridge boxes of his soldiers contained on an average only nine charges of ball and gunpowder apiece, hardly enough to engage in battle for more than ten minutes. Washington sent an urgent appeal to every town, and hearing that a ship at Bermuda had a cargo of gunpowder, American ships were despatched thither to secure it. In such straits did the army of the United Colonies go forth to war. By avoiding battles and other causes for using munitions, they not only kept their original supply, but added to it as fast as their appeals were listened to. Washington kept his lines around Boston firm. In the autumn General Gage was replaced, as British Commander-in-Chief, by Sir William Howe, whose brother Richard, Lord Howe, became

Admiral of the Fleet. But the Howes knew no way to break the strangle hold of the Americans. How Washington contrived to create the impression that he was master of the situation is one of the mysteries of his campaigning, because, although he had succeeded in making soldiers of the raw recruits and in enforcing subordination, they were still a very skittish body. They enlisted for short terms of service, and even before their term was completed, they began to hanker to go home. This caused not only inconvenience, but real difficulty. Still, Washington steadily pushed on, and in March, 1776, by a brilliant manœuvre at Dorchester Heights, he secured a position from which his cannons could bombard every British ship in Boston Harbor. On the 17th of March all those ships, together with the garrison of eight thousand, and with two thousand fugitive Loyalists, sailed off to Halifax. Boston has been free from foreign enemies from that day to this.

CHAPTER V

TRENTON AND VALLEY FORGE

HOWE'S retreat from Boston freed Massachusetts and, indeed, all New England from British troops. It also gave Washington the clue to his own next move. He was a real soldier and therefore his instinct told him that his next objective must be the enemy's army. Accordingly he prepared to move his own troops to New York. He passed through Providence, Norwich, and New London, reaching New York on April 13th. Congress was then sitting in Philadelphia and he was requested to visit it.

He spent a fortnight during May in Philadelphia where he had conferences with men of all kinds and seems to have been particularly impressed, not to say shocked, by the lack of harmony which he discovered. The members of the Congress, although they were ostensibly devoting themselves to the common affairs of the United Colonies, were really intriguing each for the interests of his special colony or section. Washington thought this an ominous sign, as indeed it was, for since the moment when he joined the Revolution he threw off all local affiliation. He did his utmost to perform his duty, clinging as long as he could to the hope that there would be no final break with England. Throughout the winter, however, from almost every part of the country the demands of the Colonists for independence became louder and more urgent and these he heard repeated and discussed during his visit to the Congress. On May 31st he wrote his brother John Augustine Washington:

Things have come to that pass now, as to convince us, that we have nothing more to expect from the justice of Great Britain; also, that she is capable of the most delusive acts; for I am satisfied, that no commissioners ever were designed, except Hessians and other foreigners; and that the idea was only to deceive and throw us off our guard. The first has been too effectually accomplished, as many members of Congress, in short, the representation of whole provinces, are still feeding themselves upon the dainty food of reconciliation; and though they will not allow, that the expectation of it has any influence upon their judgment, (with respect to their preparations for defence,) it is but too obvious, that it has an operation upon every part of their conduct, and is a clog to their proceedings. It is not in the nature of things to be otherwise; for no man, that entertains a hope of seeing this dispute speedily and equitably adjusted by commissioners, will go to the same expense and run the same hazards to prepare for the worst event, as he who believes that he must conquer, or submit to unconditional terms, and its concomitants, such as confiscation, hanging, etc. etc.[1]

[1] Ford, IV, 106.

The Hessians to whom Washington alludes were German mercenaries hired by the King of England from two or three of the princelings of Germany. These Hessians turned a dishonest penny by fighting in behalf of a cause in which they took no immediate interest or even knew what it was about. During the course of the Revolution there were thirty thousand Hessians in the British armies in America, and, as their owners, the German princelings, received £5 apiece for them it was a profitable arrangement for those phlegmatic, corpulent, and braggart personages. The Americans complained that the Hessians were brutal and tricky fighters; but in reality they merely carried out the ideals of their German Fatherland which remained behind the rest of Europe in its ideals of what was fitting in war. Being uncivilized, they could not be expected to follow the practice of civilized warfare.

When Washington returned to his headquarters in New York, he left the Congress in Philadelphia simmering over the question of Independence. Almost simultaneously with Washington's return came the British fleet under Howe, which passed Sandy Hook and sailed up New York Harbor. He brought an army of twenty-five thousand men. Washington's force was nominally nineteen thousand men, but it was reduced to not more than ten thousand by the detachment of several thousand to guard Boston and of several thousand more to take part in the struggle in Canada, besides thirty-six hundred sick. The Colonists clung as if by obsession to their project of capturing Quebec. The death of Montgomery and the discomfiture of Benedict Arnold, which really gave a quietus to the success of the expedition, did not suffice to crush it. Only too evident was it that Quebec could be taken. Canada would fall permanently into American control, and cease to be a constant menace and the recruiting ground for new expeditions against the central Colonies.

August was drawing to a close when the two armies were in a position to begin fighting. The British, who had originally camped upon Staten Island where Nature provided them with a shelter from attack, had now moved across the bay to Long Island. There General Sullivan, having lost eleven or twelve hundred men, was caught between two fires and compelled to surrender with the two thousand or more of his army which remained after the attack of the British. Washington watched the disaster from Brooklyn, but was unable to detach any regiments to bring aid to Sullivan, as it now became clear to him that his whole army on Long Island might easily be cut off. He decided to retreat from

the island. This he did on August 29th, having com-
mandeered every boat that he could find. He fer-
ried his entire force across to the New York side
with such secrecy and silence that the British did not
notice that they were gone. A heavy fog, which settled over the water during the night, greatly aided
the adventure. The result of the Battle of Long
Island gave the British great exultation and cor-
respondingly depressed the Americans. On the
preceding fourth of July they had declared their
Independence; they were no longer Colonies but
independent States bound together by a common
interest. They felt all the more keenly that in this
first battle after their Independence they should be
so ignominiously defeated. They might have taken
much comfort in the thought that had Howe sur-
prised them on their midnight retreat across the
river, he might have captured most of the American
army and probably have ended the war. Washington's disaster sprang not from his incompetence, but
from his inadequate resources. The British out-
numbered him more than two to one and they had
control of the water; an advantage which he could
not offset. One important fact should not be forgotten: New York, both City and State, had been
notoriously Loyalist — that is, pro-British — ever
since the troubles between the Colonists and the

British grew angry. Governor Tryon, the Governor of the State, made no secret of his British preferences; indeed, they were not preferences at all, but downright British acts.

Having won the Battle of Long Island, Lord Howe thought the time favorable for acting in his capacity as a peacemaker, because he had come over with authority to negotiate a peaceful settlement of the Colonists' quarrel. He appealed, therefore, to the Congress of Philadelphia, which appointed a committee of three — Benjamin Franklin, John Adams, and Edward Rutledge to confer with Lord Howe. The conference, which exhibited the shrewd quality of John Adams and of Franklin, the politeness of Rutledge, and the studied urbanity of Lord Howe, simply showed that there was no common ground on which they could come to an agreement. The American Commissioners returned to Philadelphia and Lord Howe to New York City and there were no further attempts at peacemaking.

Having brought his men to New York, Washington may well have debated what to do next. The general opinion seemed to be that New York must be defended at all costs. Whether Washington approved of this plan, I find it hard to say. Perhaps he felt that if the American army could hold its own on Manhattan for several weeks, it would be put into better discipline and prepared either to risk a battle with the British, or to retreat across the Hudson toward New Jersey. He decided that for the moment at least he would station his army on the heights of Harlem. From the house of Colonel Morris, where he made his headquarters, he wrote on September 4, 1776, to the President of the Congress: "We are now, as it were, upon the eve of another dissolution of our army." The term of service of most of the soldiers under Washington would expire at the end of the year, and he devoted the greater part of the letter to showing up the evils of the military system existing in the American army.

A soldier [he said] reasoned with upon the goodness of the cause he is engaged in, and the inestimable rights he is contending for, hears you with patience, and acknowledges the truth of your observations, but adds that it is of no more importance to him than to others. The officer makes you the same reply, with this further remark, that his pay will not support him and he cannot ruin himself and family to serve his country, when every member of the community is equally interested, and benefited by his labors. The few, therefore, who act upon principles of disinterestedness, comparatively speaking, are no more than a drop in the ocean.

It becomes evident to me then, that, as this contest is not likely to be the work of a day, as the war must be carried on systematically, and to do it you must have good officers, there are in my judgment no other possible means to obtain them but by establishing your army upon a permanent footing and giving your officers good pay. This will induce gentlemen and men of character to engage; and, till the bulk of your officers is composed of such persons as are actuated by principles of honor and a spirit of enterprise, you have little to expect from them.[1]

Washington proceeds to argue that the soldiers ought not to be engaged for a shorter time than the duration of the war, that they ought to have better pay and the offer of a hundred or a hundred and fifty acres of land. Officers' pay should be increased in proportion. "Why a captain in the Continental service should receive no more than five shillings currency per day for performing the same duties that an officer of the same rank in the British service receives ten shillings for, I never could conceive." He further speaks strongly against the employment of militia — "to place any dependence upon [it] is assuredly resting upon a broken staff."

Washington wrote thus frankly to the Congress which seems to have read his doleful reports without really being stimulated, as it ought to have been, by a determination to remove their causes. Probably the delegates came to regard the jeremiads as a matter of course and assumed that Washington would pull through somehow. Very remarkable is it that the Commander-in-Chief of any army in such a struggle should have expressed himself as he did,

[1] Ford, IV, 440.

bluntly, in regard to its glaring imperfections. Doing this, however, he managed to hold the loyalty and spirit of his men. In the American Civil War, McClellan contrived to infatuate his troops with the belief that his plans were perfect, and that only the annoying fact that the Confederate generals planned better caused him to be defeated; and yet to his obsessed soldiers defeat under McClellan was more glorious than victory under Lee or Stonewall Jackson. I take it that Washington's frankness simply reflected his passion for veracity, which was the cornerstone of his character. The strangest fact of all was that it did not lessen his popularity or discourage his troops.

To his intimates Washington wrote with even more unreserve. Thus he says to Lund Washington (30th September):

In short, such is my situation that if I were to wish the bitterest curse to an enemy on this side of the grave, I should put him in my stead with my feelings; and yet I do not know what plan of conduct to pursue. I see the impossibility of serving with reputation, or doing any essential service to the cause by continuing in command, and yet I am told that if I quit the command, inevitable ruin will follow from the distraction that will ensue. In confidence I tell you that I never was in such an unhappy, divided state since I was born. To lose all comfort and happiness on the one hand, whilst I am fully persuaded that under such a system of management as has been adopted, I cannot have the least chance for reputation, nor those allowances made which the nature of the case requires; and to be told, on the other, that if I leave the service all will be lost, is, at the same time that I am bereft of every peaceful moment, distressing to a degree. But I will be done with the subject, with the precaution to you that it is not a fit one to be publicly known or discussed. If I fall, it may not be amiss that these circumstances be known, and declaration made in credit to the justice of my character. And if the men will stand by me (which by the by I despair of), I am resolved not to be forced from this ground while I have life; and a few days will determine the point, if the enemy should not change their place of operations; for they certainly will not — I am sure they ought not — to waste the season that is now fast advancing, and must be precious to them.[1]

The British troops almost succeeded in surrounding Washington's force north of Harlem. Washington retreated to White Plains, where, on October 28th, the British, after a severe loss, took an outpost and won what is called the "Battle of White Plains." Henceforward Washington's movements resembled too painfully those of the proverbial toad under the harrow; and yet in spite of Lord Howe's efforts to crush him, he succeeded in escaping into New Jersey with a small remnant — some six thousand men — of his original army. The year 1776 thus closed in disaster which seemed to be irremediable. It showed that the British, having awakened to the magnitude

[1] Ford, IV, 458.

of their task, were able to cope with it. Having a comparatively unlimited sea-power, they needed only to embark their regiments, with the necessary provisions and ammunition, on their ships and send them across the Atlantic, where they were more than a match for the nondescript, undisciplined, ill-equipped, and often badly nourished Americans. The fact that at the highest reckoning hardly a half of the American people were actively in favor of Independence, is too often forgotten. But from this fact there followed much lukewarmness and inertia in certain sections. Many persons had too little imagination or were too sordidly bound by their daily ties to care. As one planter put it: "My business is to raise tobacco, the rest does n't concern me."

Over the generally level plains of New Jersey, George Washington pushed the remnant of the army that remained to him. He had now hardly five thousand men, but they were the best, most seasoned, and in many respects the hardiest fighters. In addition to the usual responsibility of warfare, of feeding his troops, finding quarters for them, and of directing the line of march, he had to cope with wholesale desertions and to make desperate efforts to raise money and to persuade some of those troops, whose term was expiring, to stay on. His general plan now was to come near enough to the British centre and to watch its movements. The British had fully twenty-five thousand men who could be centred at a given point. This centre was now Trenton, and the objective of the British was so plainly Philadelphia that the Continental Congress, after voting to remain in permanence there, fled as quietly as possible to Baltimore. On December 18th Washington wrote from the camp near the Falls of Trenton to John Augustine Washington:

If every nerve is not strained to recruit the new army with all possible expedition, I think the game is pretty near up, owing, in great measure, to the insidious acts of the Enemy, and disaffection of the Colonies before mentioned, but principally to the accursed policy of short enlistments, and placing too great a dependence on the militia, the evil consequences of which were foretold fifteen months ago, with a spirit almost Prophetic. ... You can form no idea of the perplexity of my situation. No man, I believe, ever had a greater choice of difficulties, and less means to extricate himself from them. However, under a full persuasion of the justice of our cause, I cannot entertain an idea that it will finally sink, though it may remain for some time under a cloud.[1]

Washington stood with his forlorn little army on the west bank of the Delaware above Trenton. He had information that the British had stretched their line very far and thin to the east of the town. Sep-

[1] Ford, v, 111.

arating his forces into three bodies, he commanded one of these himself, and during the night of Christmas he crossed the river in boats. The night was stormy and the crossing was much interrupted by floating cakes of ice; in spite of which he landed his troops safely on the eastern shore. They had to march nine miles before they reached Trenton, taking Colonel Rall and his garrison of Hessians by surprise. More than a thousand surrendered and were quickly carried back over the river into captivity.

The prestige of the Battle of Trenton was enormous. For the first time in six months Washington had beaten the superior forces of the British and beaten them in a fortified town of their own choosing. The result of the victory was not simply military; it quickly penetrated the population of New Jersey which had been exasperatingly Loyalist, had sold the British provisions, and abetted their intrigues. Now the New Jersey people suddenly bethought them that they might have chosen the wrong side after all. This feeling was deepened in them a week later when, at Princeton, Washington suddenly fell upon and routed several British regiments. By this success he cleared the upper parts of New Jersey of British troops, who were shut once more within the limits of New York City and Long Island.

WASHINGTON AT THE BATTLE OF TRENTON
By Colonel John Trumbull

In January, 1777, no man could say that the turning-point in the American Revolution had been passed. There were still to come long months, and years even, of doubt and disillusion and suffering; the agony of Valley Forge; the ignominy of betrayal; and the slowly gnawing pain of hope deferred. But the fact, if men could have but seen it, was clear — Trenton and Princeton were prophetic of the end. And what was even clearer was the supreme importance of George Washington. Had he been cut off after Princeton or had he been forced to retire through accident, the Revolution would have slackened, lost head and direction, and spent itself among thinly parcelled rivulets without strength to reach the sea. Washington was a Necessary Man. Without him the struggle would not then have continued. Sooner or later America would have broken free from England, but he was indispensable to the liberty and independence of the Colonies then. This thought brooded over him at all times, not to make him boastful or imperious, but to impress him with a deeper awe, and to impress also his men with the supreme importance of his life to them all. They grew restive when, at Princeton, forgetful of self, he faced a volley of muskets only thirty feet away. One of his officers wrote after the Trenton campaign:

Our army love their General very much, but they have one thing against him, which is the little care he takes of himself in any action. His personal bravery, and the desire he has of animating his troops by example, makes him fearless of danger. This occasions us much uneasiness. But Heaven, which has hitherto been his shield, I hope will still continue to guard so valuable a life.[1]

Robert Morris, who had already achieved a very important position among the Patriots of New York, wrote to Washington:

Heaven, no doubt for the noblest purposes, has blessed you with a firmness of mind, steadiness of countenance, and patience in sufferings, that give you infinite advantages over other men. This being the case, you are not to depend on other people's exertions being equal to your own. One mind feeds and thrives on misfortunes by finding resources to get the better of them; another sinks under their weight, thinking it impossible to resist; and, as the latter description probably includes the majority of mankind, we must be cautious of alarming them.

Washington doubtless thanked Morris for his kind advice about issuing reports which had some streaks of the rainbow and less truth in them. He did not easily give up his preference for truth.

Common prudence [he said] dictates the necessity of duly attending to the circumstances of both armies, before the style of conquerors is assumed by either; and

---

[1] Hapgood, 171.

I am sorry to add, that this does not appear to be the case with us; nor is it in my power to make Congress fully sensible of the real situation of our affairs, and that it is with difficulty (if I may use the expression) that I can, by every means in my power, keep the life and soul of this army together. In a word, when they are at a distance, they think it is but to say, Presto begone, and everything is done. They seem not to have any conception of the difficulty and perplexity attending those who are to execute.

After the Battle of Princeton, Washington drew his men off to the Heights of Morristown where he established his winter quarters. The British had gone still farther toward New York City. Both sides seemed content to enjoy a comparative truce until spring should come with better weather; but true to his characteristic of being always preparing something, Howe had several projects in view, any one of which might lead to important activity. If ever a war was fought at long range, that war was the American Revolution. Howe received his orders from the War Office in London. Every move was laid down; no allowance was made for the change which unforeseeable contingencies might render necessary; the young Under-Secretaries who carefully drew up the instructions in London knew little or nothing about the American field of operations and simply relied upon the fact that their callipers showed that it was so many miles between Point X and Point Y and that the distance should ordinarily be covered in so many hours.

With Washington himself the case was hardly better. There were few motions that he could make of his own free will. He had to get authority from the Continental Congress at Philadelphia. The Congress was not made up of military experts and in many cases it knew nothing about the questions he asked. The members of the Congress were talkers, not doers, and they sometimes lost themselves in endless debate and sometimes they seemed quite to forget the questions Washington put to them. We find him writing in December to beg them to reply to the urgent question which he had first asked in the preceding October. He was scrupulous not to take any step which might seem dictatorial. The Congress and the people of the country dreaded military despotism. That dread made them prefer the evil system of militia and the short-term enlistments to a properly organized standing army. To their fearful imagination the standing army would very quickly be followed by the man on horseback and by hopeless despotism.

The Olympians in London who controlled the larger issues of war and peace whispered to the young gentlemen in the War Office to draw up plans for the invasion, during the summer of 1777, of the lower Hudson by British troops from Canada. General Burgoyne should march down and take Ticonderoga and then proceed to Albany. There he could meet a smaller force under Colonel St. Leger coming from Oswego and following the Mohawk River. A third army under Sir William Howe could ascend the Hudson and meet Burgoyne and St. Leger at the general rendezvous — Albany. It was a brave plan, and when Burgoyne started with his force of eight thousand men high hopes flushed the British hearts. These hopes seemed to be confirmed when a month later Burgoyne took Ticonderoga. The Americans attributed great importance to this place, an importance which might have been justified at an earlier time, but which was now really passed, and it proved of little value to Burgoyne. Pursuing his march southward, he found himself entangled in the forest and he failed to meet boats which were to ferry him over the streams.

The military operations during the summer and autumn of 1777 might well cause the Americans to exult. The British plan of sending three armies to clear out the forces which guarded or blocked the road from Canada to the lower Hudson burst like a bubble. The chief contingent of 8000 men, under General Burgoyne, seems to have strayed from its route and to have been in need of food. Hearing that there were supplies at Bennington, Burgoyne turned aside to that place. He little suspected the mettle of John Stark and of his Green Mountain volunteers. Their quality was well represented by Stark's address to his men: "They are ours to-night, or Molly Stark is a widow." He did not boast. By nightfall he had captured all of Burgoyne's men who were alive (August 16, 1777).

Only one reverse marred the victories of the summer. This was at Oriskany in August, 1777. An American force of 400 or 500 men fell into an ambush, and its leader, General Herkimer, though mortally wounded, refused to retire, but continued to give directions to the end. Oriskany was reputed to be the most atrocious fight of the Revolution. Joseph Brant, the Mohawk chief, led the Indians, who were allies of the English.

In spite of this, Burgoyne seemed to lose resolution, uncertain whither to turn. He instinctively groped for a way that would take him down the Hudson and bring him to Albany, where he was to meet British reënforcements. But he missed his bearings and found himself near Saratoga. Here General Gates confronted him with an army larger than his own in regulars. On October 7th they fought a battle, which the British technically claimed as a victory, as they were not driven from their position, but it left them virtually hemmed in without a line of escape. Burgoyne waited several days irresolute. He hoped that something favorable to him might turn up. He had a lurking hope that General Clinton was near by, coming to his rescue. He wavered, gallant though he was, and would not give the final order of desperation — to cut their way through the enemy lines. Instead of that he sought a truce with Gates, and signed the Convention of Saratoga (October 17th), by which he surrendered his army with the honors of war, and it was stipulated that they should be sent to England by English ships and paroled against taking any further part in the war.

The victory of Saratoga had much effect on America; it reverberated through Europe. Only the peculiar nature of the fighting in America prevented it from being decisive. Washington himself had never dared to risk a battle which, if he were defeated in it, would render it impossible for him to continue the war. The British, on the other hand, spread over much ground, and the destruction of one of their armies would not necessarily involve the loss of all. So it was now; Burgoyne's surrender did little to relieve the pressure on Washington's troops on the Hudson, but it had a vital effect across the sea.

Since the first year of the war the Americans had

hoped to secure a formal alliance with France against England, and among the French who favored this scheme there were several persons of importance. Reasons were easily found to justify such an alliance. The Treaty of Paris in 1763 had dispossessed France of her colonies in America and had left her inferior to England in other parts of the world. Here was her chance to take revenge. The new King, Louis XVI, had for Foreign Minister Count de Vergennes, a diplomat of some experience, who warmly urged supporting the cause of the American Colonists. He had for accomplice Beaumarchais, a nimble-witted playwright and seductive man of the world who talked very persuasively to the young King and many others.

The Americans on their side had not been inactive, and early in 1776 Silas Deane, a member of Congress from Connecticut, was sent over to Paris with the mission to do his utmost to cement the friendship between the American Colonies and France. Deane worked to such good purpose that by October, 1776, he had sent clothing for twenty thousand men, muskets for thirty thousand and large quantities of ammunition. A fictitious French house, which went by the name of Hortalaz et Cie, acted as agent and carried on the necessary business from Paris. By this time military adventurers in large numbers be-

gan to flock to America to offer their swords to the
rebellious Colonials. Among them were a few — de
Kalb, Pulaski, Steuben, and Kosciuszko — who did
good service for the struggling young rebels, but most
of them were worthless adventurers and marplots.

Almost any American in Paris felt himself authorized to give a letter of introduction to any Frenchman or other European who wished to try his fortunes in America. One of the notorious cases was
that of a French officer named Ducoudray, who
brought a letter from Deane purporting to be an
agreement that Ducoudray should command the
artillery of the Continental army with the rank and
pay of a major-general. Washington would take no
responsibility for this appointment, which would
have displaced General Knox, a hardy veteran, an
indefectible patriot, and Washington's trusted friend.
When the matter was taken up by the Congress,
the demand was quickly disallowed. The absurdity
of allowing Silas Deane or any other American in
Paris, no matter how meritorious his own services
might be, to assign to foreigners commissions of high
rank in the American army was too obvious to be
debated.

To illustrate the character of Washington's mis-
cellaneous labors in addition to his usual household
care of the force under him, I borrow a few items

from his correspondence. I borrow at random, the time being October, 1777, when the Commander-in-Chief is moving from place to place in northern New Jersey, watching the enemy and avoiding an engagement. A letter comes from Richard Henry Lee, evidently intended to sound Washington, in regard to the appointment of General Conway to a high command in the American army. Washington replies with corroding veracity.

[Matuchin Hill, 17 October, 1777.] If there is any truth in the report that Congress hath appointed . . . Brigadier Conway a Major-general in this army, it will be as unfortunate a measure as ever was adopted. I may add, (and I think with truth) that it will give a fatal blow to the existence of the army. Upon so interesting a subject, I must speak plain. The duty I owe my country, the ardent desire I have to promote its true interests, and justice to individuals, requires this of me. General Conway's merit, then, as an officer, and his importance in this army, exists more in his imagination, than in reality. For it is a maxim with him, to leave no service of his own untold, nor to want anything, which is to be obtained by importunity.[1]

It does not appear that Lee fished for letters of introduction for himself or any of his friends after this experiment. He needed no further proof that George Washington had the art of sending *complete* answers.[2]

[1] Ford, VI, 121.
[2] For the end of Conway and his cabal see *post*, 112, 113.

On October 25, 1777, desertions being frequent among the officers and men, Washington issued this circular to Pulaski and Colonels of Horse:

I am sorry to find that the liberty I granted to the light dragoons of impressing horses near the enemy's line has been most horribly abused and perverted into a mere plundering scheme. I intended nothing more than that the horses belonging to the disaffected in the neighborhood of the British Army, should be taken for the use of the dismounted dragoons, and expected, that they would be regularly reported to the Quartermaster General, that an account might be kept of the number and the persons from whom they were taken, in order to a future settlement. — Instead of this, I am informed that under pretence of the authority derived from me, they go about the country plundering whomsoever they are pleased to denominate tories, and converting what they get to their own private profit and emolument. This is an abuse that cannot be tolerated; and as I find the license allowed them, has been made a sanction for such mischievous practices, I am under the necessity of recalling it altogether. You will therefore immediately make it known to your whole corps, that they are not under any pretence whatever to meddle with the horses or other property of any inhabitant whatever on pain of the severest punishment, for they may be assured as far as it depends upon me that military execution will attend all those who are caught in the like practice hereafter.[1]

One finds nothing ambiguous in this order to Pulaski and the Colonels of Horse. A more timid commander would have hesitated to speak so curtly

[1] Ford, VI, 141.

at a time when the officers and men of his army were deserting at will; but to Washington discipline was discipline, and he would maintain it, cost what it might, so long as he had ten men ready to obey him.

Passing over three weeks we find Washington writing from Headquarters on November 14th to Sir William Howe, the British Commander-in-Chief, in regard to the maltreatment of prisoners and to proposals of exchanging officers on parole.

I must also remonstrate against the maltreatment and confinement of our officers — this, I am informed, is not only the case of those in Philadelphia, but of many in New York. Whatever plausible pretences may be urged to authorize the condition of the former, it is certain but few circumstances can arise to justify that of the latter. I appeal to you to redress these several wrongs; and you will remember, whatever hardships the prisoners with us may be subjected to will be chargeable on you. At the same time it is but justice to observe, that many of the cruelties exercised towards prisoners are said to proceed from the inhumanity of Mr. Cunningham, provost-martial, without your knowledge or approbation.[1]

The letter was sufficiently direct for Sir William to understand it. If these extracts were multiplied by ten they would represent more nearly the mass of questions which came daily to Washington for decision. The decision had usually to be made in haste

[1] Ford, VI, 195.

MOUNT VERNON

and always with the understanding that it would not only settle the question immediately involved, but it would serve as precedent.

The victory of Saratoga gave a great impetus to the party in France which wished Louis XVI to come out boldly on the side of the Americans in their war with the British. The King was persuaded. Vergennes also secured the coöperation of Spain with France, for Spain had views against England, and she agreed that if a readjustment of sovereignty were coming in America, it would be prudent for her to be on hand to press her own claims. On February 6, 1778, the treaty between France and America was signed.[1] Long before this, however, a young French enthusiast who proved to be the most conspicuous of all the foreign volunteers, the Marquis de Lafayette, had come over with magnificent promises from Silas Deane. On being told, however, that the Congress found it impossible to ratify Deane's promises, he modestly requested to enlist in the army without pay. Washington at once took a fancy to him and insisted on his being a member of the Commander's family.

While Burgoyne's surrendered army was marching to Boston and Cambridge, to be shut up as prisoners, Washington was taking into consideration the

[1] The treaty was ratified by Congress May 4, 1778.

best place in which to pass the winter. Several
were suggested, Wilmington, Delaware, and Valley
Forge — about twenty-five miles from Philadelphia
— being especially urged upon him. Washington
preferred the latter, chiefly because it was near
enough to Philadelphia to enable him to keep watch
on the movements of the British troops in that city.

Valley Forge! One of the names in human history
associated with the maximum of suffering and distress, with magnificent patience, sacrifice, and glory.

The surrounding hills were covered with woods and
presented an inhospitable appearance. The choice was
severely criticised, and de Kalb described it as a wilderness. But the position was central and easily defended.
The army arrived there about the middle of December,
and the erection of huts began. They were built of logs
and were 14 by 15 feet each. The windows were covered
with oiled paper, and the openings between the logs
were closed with clay. The huts were arranged in streets,
giving the place the appearance of a city. It was the
first of the year, however, before they were occupied,
and previous to that the suffering of the army had become great. Although the weather was intensely cold,
the men were obliged to work at the buildings, with
nothing to support life but flour unmixed with water,
which they baked into cakes at the open fires . . . the
horses died of starvation by hundreds, and the men were
obliged to haul their own provisions and firewood. As
straw could not be found to protect the men from the
cold ground, sickness spread through their quarters with
fearful rapidity. "The unfortunate soldiers," wrote

Lafayette in after years, "they were in want of every-thing; they had neither coats, hats, shirts nor shoes; their feet and their legs froze till they became black, and it was often necessary to amputate them." ... The army frequently remained whole days without provisions, and the patient endurance of the soldiers and officers was a miracle which each moment served to renew ... while the country around Valley Forge was so impoverished by the military operations of the previous summer as to make it impossible for it to support the army. The sufferings of the latter were chiefly owing to the ineffi-ciency of Congress.[1]

No one felt more keenly than did Washington the horrors of Valley Forge. He had not believed in forming such an encampment, and from the start he denounced the neglect and incompetence of the commissions. In a letter to the President of the Con-gress on December 3, 1777, he wrote:

Since the month of July we have had no assistance from the quartermaster-general, and to want of assist-ance from this department the commissary-general charges great part of his deficiency. To this I am to add, that, notwithstanding it is a standing order, and often repeated that the troops shall always have two days' provisions by them, that they might be ready at any sudden call; yet an opportunity has scarcely ever offered of taking an advantage of the enemy, that has not either been totally obstructed or greatly impeded, on this account. And this, the great and crying evil, is not all. The soap, vinegar, and other articles allowed by Congress, we see none of, nor have we seen them, I be-

[1] F. D. Stone, *Struggle for the Delaware*, VI, ch. 5.

lieve, since the Battle of Brandywine. The first, indeed, we have now little occasion for; few men having more than one shirt, many only the moiety of one, and some none at all. In addition to which, as a proof of the little benefit received from a clothier-general, and as a further proof of the inability of an army, under the circumstances of this, to perform the common duties of soldiers, (besides a number of men confined to hospitals for want of shoes, and others in farmers' houses on the same account,) we have, by a field-return this day made, no less than two thousand eight hundred and ninety-eight men now in camp unfit for duty, because they are barefoot and otherwise naked. By the same return it appears, that our whole strength in Continental troops, including the eastern brigades, which have joined us since the surrender of General Burgoyne, exclusive of the Maryland troops sent to Wilmington, amounts to no more than eight thousand two hundred in camp fit for duty; notwithstanding which, and that since the 4th instant our numbers fit for duty, from the hardships and exposures they have undergone, particularly on account of blankets (numbers having been obliged, and still are, to sit up all night by fires, instead of taking comfortable rest in a natural and common way), have decreased near two thousand men.

We find gentlemen, without knowing whether the army was really going into winter-quarters or not (for I am sure no resolution of mine would warrant the Remonstrance), reprobating the measure as much as if they thought the soldiers were made of stocks or stones and equally insensible of frost and snow; and moreover, as if they conceived it easily practicable for an inferior army, under the disadvantages I have described ours to be, which are by no means exaggerated, to confine a superior one, in all respects well-appointed and provided

for a winter's campaign within the city of Philadelphia,
and to cover from depredation and waste the States of
Pennsylvania and Jersey. But what makes this matter
still more extraordinary in my eye is, that these very
gentlemen, — who were well apprized of the nakedness
of the troops from ocular demonstration, who thought
their own soldiers worse clad than others, and who advised me near a month ago to postpone the execution of
a plan I was about to adopt, in consequence of a resolve
of Congress for seizing clothes, under strong assurances
that an ample supply would be collected in ten days
agreeably to a decree of the State (not one article of
which, by the by, is yet come to hand) — should think a
winter's campaign, and the covering of these States from
the invasion of an enemy, so easy and practicable a
business. I can assure those gentlemen, that it is a
much easier and less distressing thing to draw remonstrances in a comfortable room by a good fireside, than
to occupy a cold, bleak hill, and sleep under frost and
snow, without clothes or blankets. However, although
they seem to have little feeling for the naked and distressed soldiers, I feel superabundantly for them, and,
from my soul, I pity those miseries, which it is neither
in my power to relieve or prevent.

It is for these reasons, therefore, that I have dwelt
upon the subject, and it adds not a little to my other
difficulties and distress to find, that much more is expected of me than is possible to be performed, and that
upon the ground of safety and policy I am obliged to
conceal the true state of the army from public view, and
thereby expose myself to detraction and calumny.[1]

Mrs. Washington, as was her custom throughout
the war, spent part of the winter with the General.

[1] Ford, VI, 259, 262.

Her brief allusions to Valley Forge would hardly lead the reader to infer the horrors that nearly ten thousand American soldiers were suffering.

"Your Mamma has not yet arrived," Washington writes to Jack Custis, "but . . . expected every hour. [My aide] Meade set off yesterday (as soon as I got notice of her intention) to meet her. We are in a dreary kind of place, and uncomfortably provided." And of this reunion Mrs. Washington wrote: "I came to this place, some time about the first of February when I found the General very well, . . . in camp in what is called the great valley on the Banks of the Schuylkill. Officers and men are chiefly in Hutts, which they say is tolerably comfortable; the army are as healthy as can be well expected in general. The General's apartment is very small; he has had a log cabin built to dine in, which has made our quarters much more tolerable than they were at first." [1]

While the Americans languished and died at Valley Forge during the winter months, Sir William Howe and his troops lived in Philadelphia not only in great comfort, but in actual luxury. British gold paid out in cash to the dealers in provisions bought full supplies from one of the best markets in America. And the people of the place, largely made up of Loyalists, vied with each other in providing entertainment for the British army. There were fashionable balls for the officers and free-and-easy revels for the soldiers. Almost at any time the British army

[1] P. L. Ford, The True George Washington, 99.

might have marched out to Valley Forge and dealt
a final blow to Washington's naked and starving
troops, but it preferred the good food and the dissi-
pations of Philadelphia; and so the winter dragged
on to spring.

Howe was recalled to England and General Sir
Henry Clinton succeeded him in the command of the
British forces. He was one of those well-upholstered
carpet knights who flourished in the British army at
that time, and was even less energetic than Howe.
We must remember, however, that the English officers who came over to fight in America had had
their earlier training in Europe, where conditions
were quite different from those here. Especially was
this true of the terrain. Occasionally a born fighter
like Wolfe did his work in a day, but this was different from spending weeks and months in battleless
campaigns. The Philadelphians arranged a farewell
celebration for General Howe which they called the
Meschianza, an elaborate pageant, said to be the
most beautiful ever seen in America, after which
General Howe and General Clinton had orders to
take their army back to New York. As much as
could be shipped on boats went that way, but the
loads that had to be carried in wagons formed a caval-
cade twelve miles long, and with the attending regiment advanced barely more than two and a half

miles a day. Washington, whose troops entered
Philadelphia as soon as the British marched out,
hung on the retreating column and at Monmouth engaged in a pitched battle, which was on the point of
being a decisive victory for the Americans when,
through the blunder of General Lee, it collapsed. The
blunder seemed too obviously intentional, but Washington appeared in the midst of the mêlée and urged
on the men to retrieve their defeat. This was the battle
of which one of the soldiers said afterwards, "At Monmouth the General swore like an angel from Heaven."
He prevented disaster, but that could not reconcile
him to the loss of the victory which had been almost
within his grasp. Those who witnessed it never forgot Washington's rage when he met Lee and asked
him what he meant and then ordered him to the rear.
Washington prepared to renew the battle on the following day, but during the night Clinton withdrew
his army, and by daylight was far on his way to the
seacoast.

Washington followed up the coast and took up his
quarters at White Plains.

CHAPTER VI

AID FROM FRANCE; TRAITORS

THIS month of July, 1778, marked two vital changes in the war. The first was the transfer by the British of the field of operations to the South. The second was the introduction of naval warfare through the coming of the French. The British seemed to desire, from the day of Concord and Lexington on, to blast every part of the Colonies with military occupation and battles. After Washington drove them out of Boston in March, 1776, they left the seaboard, except Newport, entirely free. Then for nearly three years they gave their chief attention to New York City and its environs, and to Jersey down to, and including, Philadelphia. On the whole, except for keeping their supremacy in New York, they had lost ground steadily, although they had always been able to put more men than the Americans could match in the field, so that the Americans always had an uphill fight. Part of this disadvantage was owing to the fact that the British had a fleet, often a very large fleet, which could be sent suddenly to distant points along the seacoast, much to the upsetting of the American plans.

The French Alliance, ratified during the spring,

not only gave the Americans the moral advantage of the support of a great nation, but actually the support of a powerful fleet. It opened French harbors to American vessels, especially privateers, which could there take refuge or fit out. It enabled the Continentals to carry on commerce, which before the war had been the monopoly of England. Above all it brought a large friendly fleet to American waters, which might aid the land forces and must always be an object of anxiety to the British.

Such a fleet was that under Count d'Estaing, who reached the mouth of Delaware Bay on July 8, 1778, with twelve ships of the line and four frigates. He then went to New York, but the pilots thought his heavy draught ships could not cross the bar above Sandy Hook; and so he sailed off to Newport where a British fleet worsted him and he was obliged to put into Boston for repairs. Late in the autumn he took up his station in the West Indies for the winter. This first experiment of French naval co-operation had not been crowned by victory as the Americans had hoped, but many of the other advantages which they expected from the French Alliance did ensue. The opening of the American ports to the trade of the world, and incidentally the promotion of American privateering, proved of capital assistance to the cause itself.

The summer and autumn of 1778 passed uneventfully for Washington and his army. He was not strong enough to risk any severe fighting, but wished to be near the enemy's troops to keep close watch on them and to take advantage of any mistake in their moves. We cannot see how he could have saved himself if they had attacked him with force. But that they never made the attempt was probably owing to orders from London to be as considerate of the Americans as they could; for England in that year had sent out three Peace Commissioners who bore the most seductive offers to the Americans. The Government was ready to pledge that there should never again be an attempt to quell the Colonists by an army and that they should be virtually self-governing. But while the Commissioners tried to persuade, very obviously, they did not receive any official recognition from the Congress or the local conventions, and when winter approached, they sailed back to England with their mission utterly unachieved. Rebuffed in their purpose of ending the war by conciliation, the British now resorted to treachery and corruption. I do not know whether General Sir Henry Clinton was more or less of a man of honor than the other high officers in the British army at that time. We feel instinctively loath to harbor a suspicion against the honor of these

officers; and yet, the truth demands us to declare
that some one among them engaged in the miserable
business of bribing Americans to be traitors. Where
the full guilt lies, we shall never know, but the fact
that so many of the trails lead back to General Clinton gives us a reason for a strong surmise. We have
lists drawn up at British Headquarters of the Americans who were probably approachable, and the degree of ease with which it was supposed they could be
corrupted. "Ten thousand guineas and a major-
general's commission were the price for which West
Point, with its garrison, stores, and outlying posts,
was to be placed in the hands of the British." [1] The
person with whom the British made this bargain was
Benedict Arnold, who had been one of the most
efficient of Washington's generals, and of unques-
tioned loyalty. Major John André, one of Clinton's
adjutants, served as messenger between Clinton and
Arnold. On one of these errands André, somewhat
disguised, was captured by the Americans and taken
before Washington, who ordered a court-martial at
once. Fourteen officers sat on it, including Generals
Greene, Lafayette, and Steuben. In a few hours
they brought in a verdict to the effect that "Major
André ought to be considered a spy from the enemy,
and that agreeable to the law and usage of nations,

[1] Channing, III, 305.

it is their opinion he ought to suffer death." [1]
Throughout the proceedings André behaved with
great dignity. He was a young man of sympathetic
nature. Old Steuben, familiar with the usage in the
Prussian army, said: "It is not possible to save him.
He put us to no proof, but a premeditated design
to deceive." [2]

He was sentenced to death by hanging — the
doom of traitors. He did not fear to die, but that
doom repelled him and he begged to be shot instead.
Washington, however, in view of his great crime and
as a most necessary example in that crisis, firmly
refused to commute the sentence. So, on the second
of October, 1780, André was hanged.

This is an appropriate place to refer briefly to one
of the most trying features of Washington's career
as Commander-in-Chief. From very early in the
war jealousy inspired some of his associates with a
desire to have him displaced. He was too conspicu-
ously the very head and front of the American
cause. Some men, doubtless open to dishonest suggestions, wished to get rid of him in order that they
might carry on their treasonable conspiracy with
greater ease and with a better chance of success.
Others bluntly coveted his position. Perhaps some
of them really thought that he was pursuing wrong

[1] Channing, III, 307.   [2] Ibid., 307.

methods or policy. However it may be, few command-
ers-in-chief in history have had to suffer more than
Washington did from malice and faction.

The most serious of the plots against him was the
so-called Conway Cabal, whose head was Thomas
Conway, an Irishman who had served in the French
army and had come over early in the war to the
Colonies to make his way as a soldier of fortune.
He seems to have been one of the typical Irishmen
who had no sense of truth, who was talkative and
boastful, and a mirthful companion. It happened
that Washington received a letter from one of his
friends which drew from him the following note to
Brigadier-General Conway:

A letter, which I received last night, contained the
following paragraph:
"In a letter from General Conway to General Gates
he says, 'Heaven has been determined to save your
country, or a weak General and bad counsellors would
have ruined it.'" [1]

It was characteristic of Washington that he should
tell Conway at once that he knew of the latter's
machinations. Nevertheless Washington took no
open step against him. The situation of the army at
Valley Forge was then so desperately bad that he did
not wish to make it worse, perhaps, by interjecting
into it what might be considered a matter personal

[1] Ford, vi, 180.

to himself. In the Congress also there were members who belonged to the Conway Cabal, and although it was generally known that Washington did not trust him, Congress raised his rank to that of Major-General and appointed him Inspector-General to the Army. On this Conway wrote to Washington: "If my appointment is productive of any inconvenience, or otherwise disagreeable to your Excellency, as I neither applied nor solicited for this place, I am very ready to return to France." The spice of this letter consists in the fact that Conway's disavowal was a plain lie; for he had been soliciting for the appointment "with forwardness," says Mr. Ford, "almost amounting to impudence." Conway did not enjoy his new position long. Being wounded in a duel with an American officer, and thinking that he was going to die, he wrote to Washington: "My career will soon be over, therefore justice and truth prompt me to declare my last sentiments. You are in my eyes the great and good man. May you long enjoy the love, veneration, and esteem of these states, whose liberties you have asserted by your virtues." [1] But he did not die of his wound, and in a few months he left for France. After his departure the cabal, of which he seemed to be the centre, died.

[1] Sparks, 254.

The story of this cabal is still shrouded in mystery. Whoever had the original papers either destroyed them or left them with some one who deposited them in a secret place where they have been forgotten. Persons of importance, perhaps of even greater importance than some of those who are known, would naturally do their utmost to prevent being found out.

Two other enemies of Washington had unsavory reputations in their dealings with him. One of these was General Horatio Gates, who was known as ambitious to be made head of the American army in place of Washington. Gates won the Battle of Saratoga at which Burgoyne surrendered his British army. Washington at that time was struggling to keep his army in the Highlands, where he could watch the other British forces. It was easy for any one to make the remark that Washington had not won a battle for many months, whereas Gates was the hero of the chief victory thus far achieved by the Americans. The shallow might think as they chose, however: the backbone of the country stood by Washington, and the trouble between him and Gates came to no further outbreak.

The third intriguer was General Charles Lee, who, like Gates, was an Englishman, and had served under General Braddock, being in the disaster of Fort

Duquesne. When the Revolution broke out, he took sides with the Americans, and being a glib and forth-putting person he talked himself into the repute of being a great general. The Americans proudly gave him a very high commission, in which he stood second to Washington, the Commander-in-Chief. But being taken prisoner by the British, he had no opportunity of displaying his military talents for more than two years. Then, when Washington was pursuing the enemy across Jersey, Lee demanded as his right to lead the foremost division. At Monmouth he was given the post of honor and he attacked with such good effect that he had already begun to beat the British division opposed to him when he suddenly gave strange orders which threw his men into confusion.

Lafayette, who was not far away, noticed the disorder, rode up to Lee and remarked that the time seemed to be favorable for cutting off a squadron of the British troops. To this Lee replied: "Sir, you do not know the British soldiers; we cannot stand against them; we shall certainly be driven back at first, and we must be cautious." [1] Washington himself had by this time perceived that something was wrong and galloped up to Lee in a towering passion. He addressed him words which, so far as I know, no

[1] Sparks, 275, note 1.

historian has reported, not because there was any ambiguity in them, and Lee's line was sufficiently re-formed to save the day. Lee, however, smarted under the torrent of reproof, as well he might. The next day he wrote Washington a very insulting letter. Washington replied still more hotly. Lee demanded a court-martial and was placed under arrest on three charges: "First, disobedience of orders in not attacking the enemy agreeably to repeated instructions; secondly, misbehavior before the enemy, in making an unnecessary, disorderly and shameful retreat; thirdly, disrespect to the Commander in-Chief in two letters written after the action." [1] By the ruling of the court all the charges against General Lee were sustained with the exception that the word "shameful" was omitted. Lee left the army, retired to Philadelphia, and died before the end of the Revolution. General Mifflin, another conspicuous member of the cabal, resigned at the end of the year, December, 1777. So the traducers of Washington were punished by the reactions of their own crimes.

---

[1] Sparks, 278. Sparks tells the story that when Washington administered the oath of allegiance to his troops at Valley Forge, soon after Lee had rejoined the army, the generals, standing together, held a Bible. But Lee deliberately withdrew his hand twice. Washington asked why he hesitated. He replied, "As to King George, I am ready enough to absolve myself from all allegiance to him, but I have some scruples about the Prince of Wales." (*Ibid.*, 278.)

That the malicious hostility of his enemies really troubled Washington, such a letter as the following from him to President Laurens of the Congress well indicates. He says:

I cannot sufficiently express the obligation I feel to you, for your friendship and politeness upon an occasion in which I am so deeply interested. I was not unapprized that a malignant faction had been for some time forming to my prejudice; which, conscious as I am of having ever done all in my power to answer the important purposes of the trust reposed in me, could not but give me some pain on a personal account. But my chief concern arises from an apprehension of the dangerous consequences, which intestine dissensions may produce to the common cause.

As I have no other view than to promote the public good, and am unambitious of honors not founded in the approbation of my country, I would not desire in the least degree to suppress a free spirit of inquiry into any part of my conduct, that even faction itself may deem reprehensible. The anonymous paper handed to you exhibits many serious charges, and it is my wish that it should be submitted to Congress. This I am the more inclined to, as the suppression or concealment may possibly involve you in embarrassments hereafter, since it is uncertain how many or who may be privy to the contents.

My enemies take an ungenerous advantage of me. They know the delicacy of my situation, and that motives of policy deprive me of the defence, I might otherwise make against their insidious attacks. They know I cannot combat their insinuations, however injurious, without disclosing secrets, which it is of the utmost moment to conceal. But why should I expect to be exempt from censure, the unfailing lot of an elevated station? Merit and talents, with which I can have no pretensions of rivalship, have ever been subject to it. My heart tells me, that it has been my unremitted aim to do the best that circumstances would permit; yet I may have been very often mistaken in my judgment of the means, and may in many instances deserve the imputation of error. (Valley Forge, 31 January, 1778.) [1]

Such was the sort of explanation which was wrung from the Silent Man when he explained to an intimate the secrets of his heart.

To estimate the harassing burden of these plots we must bear in mind that, while Washington had to suffer them in silence, he had also to deal every day with the Congress and with an army which, at Valley Forge, was dying slowly of cold and starvation. There was literally no direction from which he could expect help; he must hold out as long as he could and keep from the dwindling, disabled army the fact that some day they would wake up to learn that the last crumb had been eaten and that death only remained for them. On one occasion, after he had visited Philadelphia and had seen the Congress in action, he unbosomed himself about it in a letter which contained these terrible words:

If I was to be called upon to draw a picture of the times and of men, from what I have seen, and heard, and in part know, I should in one word say that idleness,

[1] Ford, VI, 353.

dissipation and extravagance seems to have laid fast hold
of most of them. That speculation — peculation — and
an insatiable thirst for riches seems to have got the better of every other consideration and almost of every
order of men. That party disputes and personal quarrels are the great business of the day whilst the momentous concerns of an empire — a great and accumulated
debt — ruined finances — depreciated money — and
want of credit (which in their consequences is the want
of everything) are but secondary considerations, and
postponed from day to day — from week to week as if
our affairs wear the most-promising aspect.

The events of 1778 made a lasting impression on
King George III. The alliance of France with the
Americans created a sort of reflex patriotism which
the Government did what it could to foster. British
Imperialism flamed forth as an ideal, one whose
purposes must be to crush the French. The most
remarkable episode was the return of the Earl of
Chatham, much broken and in precarious health, to
the King's fold. To the venerable statesman the
thought that any one with British blood in his veins
should stand by rebels of British blood, or by their
French allies, was a cause of rage. On April 7, 1778,
the great Chatham appeared in the House of Lords
and spoke for Imperialism and against the Americans and French. There was a sudden stop in his
speaking, and a moment later, confusion, as he fell
in a fit. He never spoke there again, and though he

was hurried home and cared for by the doctors as best they could, he died on the eleventh of May. At the end he reverted to the dominant ideal of his life — the supremacy of England. So his chief rival in Parliament, Edmund Burke, who shocked more than half of England by seeming to approve the nascent French Revolution, died execrating it.

The failure of the Commission on Reconciliation to get even an official hearing in America further depressed George III, and there seemed to have flitted through his unsound mind more and more frequent premonitions that England might not win after all. Having made friendly overtures, which were rejected, he now planned to be more savage than ever. In 1779 the American privateers won many victories which gave them a reputation out of proportion to the importance of the battles they fought, or the prizes they took. Chief among the commanders of these vessels was a Scotchman, John Paul Jones, who sailed the Bonhomme Richard and with two companion ships attacked the Serapis and the Scarborough, convoying a company of merchantmen off Flamborough Head. Night fell, darkness came, the Bonhomme Richard and the Serapis kept up bombarding each other at short range. During a brief pause, Pearson, the British captain, called out, "Have you struck your colors?" at which Jones

shouted back, "I have not yet begun to fight."
Before morning the Serapis surrendered and in the
forenoon the victorious Bonhomme Richard sank.
Europe rang with the exploit; not merely those easily
thrilled by a spectacular engagement, but those who
looked deeper began to ask themselves whether the
naval power that must be reckoned with was not
rising in the West.

Meanwhile, Washington kept his uncertain army
near New York. The city swarmed with Loyalists,
who at one time boasted of having a volunteer organization larger than Washington's army. These
later years seem to have been the hey-day of the
Loyalists in most of the Colonies, although the
Patriots passed severe laws against them, sequestrat-
ing their property and even banishing them. In
places like New York, where General Clinton maintained a refuge, they stayed on, hoping, as they had
done for several years, that the war would soon be
over and the King's authority restored.

In the South there were several minor fights, in
which now the British and now the Americans triumphed. At the end of December, 1779, Clinton and
Cornwallis with nearly eight thousand men went
down to South Carolina intending to reduce that
State to submission. One of Washington's lieutenants, General Lincoln, ill-advisedly thought that he

could defend Charleston. But as soon as the enemy were ready, they pressed upon him hard and he surrendered. The year ended in gloom. The British were virtually masters in the Carolinas and in Georgia. The people of those States felt that they had been abandoned by the Congress and that they were cut off from relations with the Northern States. The glamour of glory at sea which had brightened them all the year before had vanished. John Paul Jones might win a striking sea-fight, but there was no navy, nor ships enough to transport troops down to the Southern waters where they might have turned the tide of battle on shore. During the winter the British continued their marauding in the South. For lack of troops Washington was obliged to stay in his quarters near New York and feel the irksomeness of inactivity. General Nathanael Greene, a very energetic officer, next indeed to Washington himself in general estimation, commanded in the South. At the Cowpens (January 17, 1781) one of his lieutenants — Morgan, a guerilla leader — killed or captured nearly all of Tarleton's men, who formed a specially crack regiment. A little later Washington marched southward to Virginia, hoping to coöperate with the French fleet under Rochambeau and to capture Benedict Arnold, now a British Major-General, who was doing much damage in

Virginia. Arnold was too wary to be caught. Cornwallis, the second in command of the British forces, pursued Lafayette up and down Virginia. Clinton, the British Commander-in-Chief, began to feel nervous for the safety of New York and wished to detach some of his forces thither. Cornwallis led his army into Yorktown and proceeded to fortify it, so that it might resist a siege. Now at last Washington felt that he had the enemy's army within his grasp. Sixteen thousand American and French troops were brought down from the North to furnish the fighting arm he required.

Yorktown lay on the south shore of the York River, an estuary of Chesapeake Bay. On the opposite side the little town of Gloucester projected into the river. In Yorktown itself the English had thrown up two redoubts and had drawn some lines of wall. The French kept up an unremitting cannonade, but it became evident that the redoubts must be taken in order to subdue the place. Washington, much excited, took his place in the central battery along with Generals Knox and Lincoln and their staff. Those about him recognized the peril he was in, and one of his adjutants called his attention to the fact that the place was much exposed. "If you think so," said he, "you are at liberty to step back." Shortly afterward a musket ball struck the cannon

in the embrasure and rolled on till it fell at his feet.
General Knox took him by the arm. "My dear
General," he exclaimed, "we can't spare you yet."
"It is a spent ball," Washington rejoined calmly;
"no harm is done." When the redoubts were taken,
he drew a long breath and said to Knox: "The work
is done, and well done." [1] Lord Cornwallis saw that
his position was desperate, if not hopeless. And on
October 16th he made a plucky attempt to retard
the final blow, but he did not succeed. That evening
he thought of undertaking a last chance. He would
cross the York River in flatboats, land at Gloucester,
and march up the country through Virginia, Maryland, Pennsylvania, and New York. Any one who
knew the actual state of that region understood that
Cornwallis's plan was crazy; but it is to be judged as
the last gallantry of a brave man. During the night
he put forth on his flatboats, which were driven out
of their course and much dispersed by untoward
winds. They had to return to Yorktown by morning,
and at ten o'clock Cornwallis ordered that a parley
should be beaten. Then he despatched a flag of
truce with a letter to Washington proposing cessa-
tion of hostilities for twenty-four hours. Washington
knew that British ships were on their way from New
York to bring relief and he did not wish to grant so

[1] Irving, IV, 378.

much delay. He, therefore, proposed that the formal British terms should be sent to him in writing; upon which he would agree to a two hours' truce. It was the morning of the 19th of October that the final arrangement was made. Washington, on horseback, attended by his staff, headed the American line. His troops, in worn-out uniforms, but looking happy and victorious, were massed near him. Count Rochambeau, with his suite, held place on the left of the road, the French troops all well-uniformed and equipped; and they marched on the field with a military band playing — the first time, it was said, that this had been known in America. "About two o'clock the garrison sallied forth and passed through with shouldered arms, slow and solemn steps, colors cased, and drums beating a British march." [1] General O'Hara, who led them, rode up to Washington and apologized for the absence of Lord Cornwallis, who was indisposed. Washington pointed O'Hara to General Lincoln, who was to receive the submission of the garrison. They were marched off to a neighboring field where they showed a sullen and dispirited demeanor and grounded their arms so noisily and carelessly that General Lincoln had to reprove them.

With little delay Washington went back to the

[1] Irving, IV, 383.

North with his army, expecting to see the first fruits of the capitulation. There were nearly seventeen thousand Allied troops at Yorktown of whom three thousand were militia of Virginia. The British force under Cornwallis numbered less than eight thousand men.

Months were required before the truce between the two belligerents resulted in peace. But the people of America hailed the news of Yorktown as the end of the war. They had hardly admitted to themselves the gravity of the task while the war lasted, and being now relieved of immediate danger, they gave themselves up to surprising insouciance. A few among them who thought deeply, Washington above all, feared that the British might indulge in some surprise which they would find it hard to repel.

But the American Revolution was indeed ended, and the American Colonies of 1775 were indeed independent and free. Even in the brief outline of the course of events which I have given, it must appear that the American Revolution was almost the most hare-brained enterprise in history. After the first days of Lexington and Concord, when the farmers and country-folk rushed to the centres to check the British invaders, the British had almost continuously a large advantage in position and in number of troops. And in those early days the Colonists fought, not for Independence, but for the traditional rights which the British Crown threatened to take from them. Now they had their freedom, but what a freedom! There were thirteen unrelated political communities bound together now only by the fact of having been united in their common struggle against England. Each had adopted a separate constitution, and the constitutions were not uniform nor was there any central unifying power to which they all looked up and obeyed. The vicissitudes of the war, which had been fought over the region of twelve hundred miles of coast, had proved the repellent differences of the various districts. The slave-breeder and the slave-owner of Virginia and the States of the South had little in common with the gnarled descendants of the later Puritans in New England. What principle could be found to knit them together? The war had at least the advantage of bringing home to all of them the evils of war which they all instinctively desired to escape. The numbers of the disaffected, particularly of the Loyalists who openly sided with the King and with the British Government, were much larger than we generally suppose, and they not only gave much direct help and comfort to the enemy, but also much indirect and insidious aid. In the great cities like New York and

Philadelphia they numbered perhaps two fifths of the total population, and, as they were usually the rich and influential people, they counted for more than their showing in the census. How could they ever be unified in the American Republic? How many of them, like the traitorous General Charles Lee, would confess that, although they were willing to pass by George III as King, they still felt devotion and loyalty to the Prince of Wales?

Some of those who had leaned toward Loyalism, to be on what they supposed would prove the winning side, quickly forgot their lapse and were very enthusiastic in acclaiming the Patriotic victory. Those Irreconcilables who had not already fled did so at once, leaving their property behind them to be confiscated by the Government. On only one point did there seem to be unanimity and accord. That was that the dogged prosecution of the war and the ultimate victory must be credited to George Washington. Others had fought valiantly and endured hardships and fatigues and gnawing suspense, but without him, who never wavered, they could not have gone on. He had among them some able lieutenants, but not one who, had he himself fallen out of the command by wound or sickness for a month, could have taken his place. The people knew this and they now paid him in honor and gratitude for what he had done for them. If there were any members of the old cabal, any envious rivals, they either held their peace or spoke in whispers. The masses were not yet weary of hearing Aristides called the Just.

CHAPTER VII

WASHINGTON RETURNS TO PEACE

NEARLY two years elapsed before the real settlement of the war. The English held New York City, Charleston, and Savannah, the strong garrisons. It seemed likely that they would have been glad to arrange the terms of peace sooner, but there was much inner turmoil at home. The men who, through thick and thin, had abetted the King in one plan after another to fight to the last ditch had nothing more to propose. Lord North, when he heard of the surrender of Yorktown, almost shrieked, "My God! It is all over; it is all over!" and was plunged in gloom. A new ministry had to be formed. Lord North had been succeeded by Rockingham, who died in July, 1782, and was followed by Shelburne, supposed to be rather liberal, but to share King George's desire to keep down the Whigs. Negotiations over the terms of peace were carried on with varying fortune for more than a year. John Adams, John Jay, and Benjamin Franklin were the American Peace Commissioners. The preliminaries between Great Britain and America were signed on December 30, 1782, and with France and Spain nearly two months later. The Dutch held out still longer into 1783. Washington, at his Headquarters in Newburgh, New York, had been awaiting the news of peace, not lazily, but planning for a new campaign and meditating upon the various projects which might be undertaken. To him the news of the actual signing of the treaty came at the end of March. He replied at once to Theodorick Bland; a letter which gave his general views in regard to the needs and rights of the army before it should be disbanded:

It is now the bounden duty of every one to make the blessings thereof as diffusive as possible. Nothing would so effectually bring this to pass as the removal of those local prejudices which intrude upon and embarrass that great line of policy which alone can make us a free, happy and powerful People. Unless our Union can be fixed upon such a basis as to accomplish these, certain I am we have toiled, bled and spent our treasure to very little purpose. We have now a National character to establish, and it is of the utmost importance to stamp favorable impressions upon it; let justice be then one of its characteristics, and gratitude another. Public creditors of every denomination will be comprehended in the first; the Army in a particular manner will have a claim to the latter; to say that no distinction can be made between the claims of public creditors is to declare that there is no difference in circumstances; or that the services of all men are equally alike. This Army is of near eight years' standing, six of which they have spent in the Field without any other shelter from the inclemency of the seasons than Tents, or such Houses as they could build for themselves without expense to the public. They have encountered hunger, cold and nakedness. They have fought many Battles and bled freely. They have lived without pay and in consequence of it, officers as well as men have subsisted upon their Rations.

They have often, very often, been reduced to the necessity of eating Salt Porke, or Beef not for a day, or a week only but months together without Vegetables or money to buy them; or a cloth to wipe on.

Many of them do better, and to dress as Officers have contracted heavy debts or spent their patrimonies. The first see the Doors of gaols open to receive them, whilst those of the latter are shut against them. Is there no discrimination then — no extra exertion to be made in favor of men in these peculiar circumstances, in the event of their military dissolution? Or, if no worse cometh of it, are they to be turned adrift soured and discontented, complaining of the ingratitude of their Country, and under the influence of these passions to become fit subjects for unfavorable impressions, and unhappy dissentions? For permit me to add, tho every man in the Army feels his distress — it is not every one that will reason to the cause of it.

I would not from the observations here made, be understood to mean that Congress should (because I know they cannot, nor does the army expect it) pay the full arrearages due to them till Continental or State funds are established for the purpose. They would, from what I can learn, go home contented — nay — *thankful* to receive what I have mentioned in a more public letter of this date, and in the manner there expressed. And surely this may be effected with proper exertions. Or what possibility was there of keeping the army together, if the war had continued, when the victualls, clothing, and other expenses of it were to have been added? Another thing, Sir, (as I mean to be frank and free in my

communications on this subject,) I will not conceal
from you — it is the dissimilarity in the payments to
men in Civil and Military life. The first receive everything — the others get nothing but bare subsistence —
they ask what this is owing to? and reasons have
been assigned, which, say they, amount to this — that
men in Civil life have stronger passions and better pretensions to indulge them, or less virtue and regard for
their Country than us, — otherwise, as we are all contending for the same prize and equally interested in the
attainment of it, why do we not bear the burthen
equally? [1]

The army was indeed the incubus of the Americans. They could not fight the war without it, but
they had never succeeded in mastering the difficulties
of maintaining and strengthening it. The system of
a standing army was of course not to be thought of,
and the uncertain recruits who took its place were
mostly undisciplined and unreliable. When the exi-
gencies became pressing, a new method was resorted
to, and then the usual erosion of life in the field, the
losses by casualties and sickness, caused the numbers
to dwindle. Long ago the paymaster had ceased to
pretend to pay off the men regularly so that there
was now a large amount of back pay due them.
Largely through Washington's patriotic exhortations had they kept fighting to the end; and, with
peace upon them, they did not dare to disband be-

[1] Ford, x, 203.

cause they feared that, if they left before they were paid, they would never be paid. Washington felt that, if thousands of discontented and even angry soldiers were allowed to go back to their homes without the means of taking up any work or business, great harm would be done. The love of country, which he believed to be most important to inculcate, would not only be checked but perverted. They already had too many reasons to feel aggrieved. Why should they, the men who risked their lives in battle and actually had starved or frozen in winter quarters, go unpaid, whereas every civilian who had a post under the Government lived at least safely and healthily and was paid with fair promptitude? They felt now that their best hope for justice lay in General Washington's interest in their behalf; and that interest of his seems now one of the noblest and wisest and most patriotic of his expressions.

Washington had need to be prepared for any emergency. Thus a body of officers deliberated not only a mutiny of the army, but a *coup d'état*, in which they planned to overthrow the flimsy Federation of the thirteen States and to set up a monarchy. They wrote to Washington announcing their intention and their belief that he would make an ideal monarch. He was amazed and chagrined. He replied in part as follows, to the Colonel who had written him:

I am much at a loss to conceive what part of my conduct could have given encouragement to an address, which to me seems big with the greatest mischiefs, that can befall my country. If I am not deceived in the knowledge of myself, you could not have found a person to whom your schemes are more disagreeable. I must add, that no man possesses a more sincere wish to see ample justice done to the army than I do; and, as far as my powers and influence, in a constitutional way, extend, they shall be employed to the extent of my abilities to effect it, should there be any occasion. Let me conjure you, then, if you have any regard for your country, concern for yourself or posterity, or respect for me, to banish these thoughts from your mind and never communicate, as from yourself to any one else, a sentiment of the like nature.[1]

The turmoil of the army continued throughout the year and into the next. The so-called "Newburgh Address" set forth the quarrel of the soldiers and Washington's discreet reply. On April 19, 1783, the eighth anniversary of the first fighting at Concord, a proclamation was issued to the American army announcing the official end of all hostilities. In June Washington issued a circular letter to the Governors of the States, bidding them farewell and urging them to guard their precious country. Many of the American troops were allowed to go home on

[1] Sparks, 355.

furlough. In company with Governor Clinton, he went up the Hudson to Ticonderoga and then westward to Fort Schuyler. Being invited by Congress, which was then sitting at Annapolis, he journeyed thither. Before he left New York City arrangements were made for a formal farewell to his comrades in arms. I quote the description of it from Chief Justice Marshall's "Life of Washington":

This affecting interview took place on the 4th of December. At noon, the principal officers of the army assembled at Frances' tavern; soon after which, their beloved commander entered the room. His emotions were too strong to be concealed. Filling a glass, he turned to them and said, "with a heart full of love and gratitude, I now take leave of you; I most devoutly wish that your latter days may be as prosperous and happy, as your former ones have been glorious and honorable." Having drunk, he added, "I cannot come to each of you to take my leave, but shall be obliged to you, if each of you will come and take me by the hand." General Knox, being nearest, turned to him. Incapable of utterance, Washington grasped his hand, and embraced him. In the same affectionate manner, he took leave of each succeeding officer. In every eye was the tear of dignified sensibility; and not a word was articulated to interrupt the majestic silence and the tenderness of the scene. Leaving the room, he passed through the corps of light infantry, and walked to White hall, where a barge waited to convey him to Powles' hook (Paulus Hook). The whole company followed in mute and solemn procession, with dejected countenances, testifying feelings of delicious melancholy, which no language can describe. Having entered the barge, he turned to the company;

and waving his hat, bade them a silent adieu. They paid him the same affectionate compliment, and after the barge had left them, returned in the same solemn manner to the place where they had assembled.[1]

Marshall's description, simple but not commonplace, reminds one of Ville-Hardouin's pictures, so terse, so rich in color, of the Barons of France in the Fifth Crusade. The account once read, you can never forget that majestic, silent figure of Washington being rowed across to Paulus Hook with no sound but the dignified rhythm of the oars. Not a cheer, not a word!

His reception by Congress took place on Tuesday, the twenty-third of December, at twelve o'clock. Again I borrow from Chief Justice Marshall's account:

When the hour arrived for performing a ceremony so well calculated to recall to the mind the various interesting scenes which had passed since the commission now to be returned was granted, the gallery was crowded with spectators, and many respectable persons, among whom were the legislative and executive characters of the state, several general officers, and the consul general of France, were admitted on the floor of Congress.

The representatives of the sovereignty of the union remained seated and covered. The spectators were standing and uncovered. The General was introduced by the secretary and conducted to a chair. After a decent interval, silence was commanded, and a short pause

[1] Marshall, IV, 561.

ensued. The President (General Mifflin) then informed him that "the United States in Congress assembled were prepared to receive his communications." With a native dignity improved by the solemnity of the occasion, the General rose and delivered the following address:

"*Mr. President:*

"The great events on which my resignation depended, having at length taken place, I have now the honor of offering my sincere congratulations to Congress, and of presenting myself before them, to surrender into their hands the trust committed to me and to claim the indulgence of retiring from the service of my country.

"Happy in the confirmation of our independence and sovereignty and pleased with the opportunity afforded the United States, of becoming a respectable nation, I resign with satisfaction the appointment I accepted with diffidence; a diffidence in my abilities to accomplish so arduous a task, which, however, was superseded by a confidence in the rectitude of our cause, the support of the supreme power of the union, and the patronage of heaven.

"The successful termination of the war has verified the most sanguine expectations; and my gratitude for the interposition of Providence, and the assistance I have received from my countrymen, increases with every review of the momentous contest.

"While I repeat my obligations to the army in general, I should do injustice to my own feelings not to acknowledge in this place, the peculiar services and distinguished merits of the gentlemen who have been attached to my person during the war. It was impossible the choice of confidential officers to compose my family should have been more fortunate. Permit me, sir, to recommend in particular, those who have continued in the service to the present moment, as worthy of the favorable notice and patronage of Congress.

"I consider it as an indispensable duty to close this last act of my official life, by commending the interests of our dearest country, to the protection of Almighty God, and those who have the superintendence of them to his holy keeping.

"Having now finished the work assigned me, I retire from the great theatre of action, and bidding an affectionate farewell to this august body, under whose orders I have so long acted, I here offer my commission, and take my leave of all the employments of public life."

After advancing to the chair, and delivering his commission to the President, he returned to his place, and received standing, the answer of Congress which was delivered by the President. In the course of his remarks, General Mifflin said:

"Having defended the standard of liberty in this new world: having taught a new lesson useful to those who inflict, and to those who feel oppression, you retire from the great theatre of action, with the blessings of your fellow citizens; but the glory of your virtues will not terminate with your military command: it will continue to animate remotest ages." [1]

The meeting then broke up, and Washington departed. He went that same afternoon to Virginia and reached Mount Vernon in the evening. We can imagine with what satisfaction and gratitude he, to whom home was the dearest place in the world, returned to the home he had seen only once by chance since the beginning of the Revolution, eight years before. Probably few of those who had risen to the highest station in their country said, and felt more

[1] Marshall, IV, 563.

honestly, that they were grateful at being allowed by Fate to retire from office, than did Washington. To be relieved of responsibility, free from the hourly spur, day and night, of planning and carrying out, of trying to find food for starving soldiers, of leading forlorn hopes against the truculent enemy, must have seemed to the weary and war-worn General like a call from the Hesperides. Men of his iron nature, and of his capacity for work and joy in it, do not, of course, really delight in idleness. They may think that they crave idleness, but in reality they crave the power of going on.

It took comparatively little effort for Washington to fall into his old way of life at Mount Vernon, although there, too, much was changed. Old buildings had fallen out of repair. There were new experiments to be tried, and the general purpose to be carried out of making Mount Vernon a model place in that part of the country. Whether he would or not, he was sought for almost daily by persons who came from all parts of the United States, and from overseas. Hospitality being not merely a duty, but a passion with him, he gladly received the strangers and learned much from them. From their accounts of their interviews we see that, although he was really the most natural of men, some of them treated him as if he were some strange creature — a holy white elephant of Siam, or the Grand Lama of Tibet. Age had brought its own deductions and reservations. It does not appear that parties rode to hounds after the fox any more at Mount Vernon. And then there were the irreparable gaps that could not be filled. At Belvoir, where his neighbors the Fair-faxes, friends of a lifetime, used to live, they lived no more. One of them, more than ninety years old, had turned his face to the wall on hearing of the surrender at Yorktown. Another had gone back to England to live out his life there, true to his Tory convictions.

Washington had sincerely believed, no doubt, that he was to spend the rest of his life in dignified leisure, and especially that he would mix no more in political or public worries; but he soon found that he had deceived himself. The army, until it officially dis-banded at the end of 1783, caused him constant anxiety interspersed with fits of indignation over the indifference and inertia of the Congress, which showed no intention of being just to the soldiers. The reason for its attitude seems hard to state posi-tively. May it be that the Congress, jealous since the war began of being ruled by the man on horse-back, feared at its close to grant Washington's demands for it lest they should bring about the very thing they had feared and avoided — the creation of a military dictatorship under Washington? When Vergennes proposed to entrust to Washington a new subsidy from France, the Congress had taken umbrage and regarded such a proposal as an insult to the American Government. Should they admit that the Government itself was not sufficiently sound and trustworthy, and that, therefore, a private individual, even though he had been a leader of the Revolution, must be called into service?

From among persons pestered by this obsession, it was not surprising that the idea should spring up that Washington was at heart a believer in monarchy and that he might, when the opportunity favored, allow himself to be proclaimed king. Several years later he wrote to his trusted friend, John Jay:

I am told that even respectable characters speak of a monarchical form of government without horror. From thinking proceeds speaking; thence to acting is often but a single step. But how irrevocable and tremendous! What a triumph for our enemies to verify their predictions! What a triumph for the advocates of despotism to find, that we are incapable of governing ourselves, and that systems founded on the basis of equal liberty are merely ideal and fallacious! Would to God, that wise measures may be taken in time to avert the consequences we have but too much reason to apprehend.[1]

In the renewal of his life at Mount Vernon, Washington gave almost as much attention to the culti-

[1] Hapgood, 285.

vation of friendship as to that of his estate. He pursued with great zest the career of planter-farmer. "I think," he wrote a friend, "with you, that the life of a husbandman of all others is the most delectable. It is honorable, it is amusing, and, with judicious management, it is profitable. To see plants rise from the earth and flourish by the superior skill and bounty of the laborer fills a contemplative mind with ideas which are more easy to be conceived than expressed." [1]

The cultivation of his friendships he carried on by letters and by entertaining his friends as often as he could at Mount Vernon. To Benjamin Harrison he wrote: "My friendship is not in the least lessened by the difference, which has taken place in our political sentiments, nor is my regard for you diminished by the part you have acted." [2]

How constantly the flock of guests frequented Mount Vernon we can infer from this entry in his diary for June 30, 1785: "Dined with only Mrs. Washington which, I believe, is the first instance of it since my retirement from public life." To his young friend Lafayette he wrote without reserve in a vein of deep affection:

At length, my dear Marquis, I am become a private citizen on the banks of the Potomac; and under the

[1] Hapgood, 288.   [2] *Ibid.*, 289.

shadow of my own vine and my own fig-tree, free from the bustle of a camp, and the busy scenes of public life, I am solacing myself with those tranquil enjoyments, of which the soldier, who is ever in pursuit of fame, the statesman, whose watchful days and sleepless nights are spent in devising schemes to promote the welfare of his own, perhaps the ruin of other countries, as if this globe was insufficient for us all, and the courtier, who is always watching the countenance of his prince, in hopes of catching a gracious smile, can have very little conception. I have not only retired from all public employments, but I am retiring within myself, and shall be able to view the solitary walk, and tread the paths of private life, with heartful satisfaction. Envious of none, I am determined to be pleased with all; and this, my dear friend, being the order of my march, I will move gently down the stream of life, until I sleep with my fathers.[1]

In September, 1784, he made a journey on horseback, with a pack-train to carry his tents and food, into the Northwestern country, which had especially interested him since the early days when Fort Duquesne was the goal of his wandering. He observed very closely and his mind was filled with large imaginings of what the future would see in the development of the Northwest. Since his youth he had never lost the conviction that an empire would spring up there; only make the waterways easy and safe and he felt sure that a very large commerce would result and with it the extension of civilization. In a memorial to the legislature he urged that Vir-

[1] Hapgood, 287.

ginia was the best placed geographically of all the States to undertake the work of establishing connection with the States of the Northwest, and he suggested various details which, when acted upon later, proved to be, as Sparks remarked, "the first suggestion of the great system of internal improvements which has since been pursued in the United States."

On returning to Mount Vernon, he entertained Lafayette for the last time before he sailed for France. After he had gone, Washington wrote him this letter in which appears the affection of a friend and the reverie of an old man looking somewhat wistfully towards sunset, "and after that the dark":

In the moment of our separation, upon the road as I travelled, and every hour since, I have felt all that love, respect, and attachment for you, with which length of years, close connection, and your merits have inspired me. I often asked myself as our carriages separated, whether that was the last sight I ever should have of you? And, though I wished to say No, my fears answered Yes. I called to mind the days of my youth, and found they had long since fled to return no more; that I was now descending the hill I had been fifty-two years climbing, and that, though I was blest with a good constitution, I was of a short-lived family and might soon expect to be entombed in the mansion of my fathers. These thoughts darkened the shades, and gave a gloom to the picture, and consequently to my prospect of seeing you again.

We should not overlook the fact that Washington declined all gifts, including a donation from Virginia, for his services as General during the war. He had refused to take any pay, merely keeping a strict account of what he spent for the Government from 1775 to 1782. This amounted to over £15,000 and covered only sums actually disbursed by him for the army. Unlike Marlborough, Nelson, and Wellington, and other foreign chieftains on whom grateful countrymen conferred fortunes and high titles, Washington remains as the one great state-founder who literally *gave* his services to his country.

Sparks gives the following interesting account of the way in which Washington spent his days after his return to Mount Vernon:

His habits were uniform, and nearly the same as they had been previous to the war. He rose before the sun and employed himself in his study, writing letters or reading, till the hour of breakfast. When breakfast was over, his horse was ready at the door, and he rode to his farms and gave directions for the day to the managers and laborers. Horses were likewise prepared for his guests, whenever they chose to accompany him, or to amuse themselves by excursions into the country. Returning from his fields, and despatching such business as happened to be on hand, he went again to his study, and continued there till three o'clock, when he was summoned to dinner. The remainder of the day and the evening were devoted to company, or to recreation in the family circle. At ten he retired to rest. From these habits he seldom

deviated, unless compelled to do so by particular circumstances.[1]

This list does not include the item which Washington soon found the greatest of his burdens —
letter-writing. His correspondence increased rapidly
and to an enormous extent.

Many mistakenly think [he writes to Richard Henry
Lee] that I am retired to ease, and to that kind of tran-
quility which would grow tiresome for want of employment; but at no period of my life, not in the eight years
I served the public, have I been obliged to write so much
myself, as I have done since my retirement. . . . It is
not the letters from my friends which give me trouble,
or add aught to my perplexity. It is references to old
matters, with which I have nothing to do; applications
which often cannot be complied with; inquiries which
would require the pen of a historian to satisfy; letters of
compliment as unmeaning perhaps as they are trouble-
some, but which must be attended to; and the commonplace business which employs my pen and my time often
disagreeably. These, with company, deprive me of exercise, and unless I can obtain relief, must be productive
of disagreeable consequences.[2]

When we remember that Washington used to
write most of his letters himself, and that from boyhood his handwriting was beautifully neat, almost
like copper-plate, in its precision and elegance, we
shall understand what a task it must have been for
him to keep up his correspondence. A little later he

[1] Sparks, 389, 390.   [2] Irving, IV, 466.

employed a young New Hampshire graduate of
Harvard, Tobias Lear, who graduated in 1783, who
served him as secretary until his death, and undoubtedly lightened the epistolary cares of the General. But Washington continued to carry on much
of the letter-writing, especially the intimate, himself; and, like the Adamses and other statesmen of
that period, he kept letter-books which contained
the first drafts or copies of the letters sent.

Another source of annoyance, to which, however,
he resigned himself as contentedly as he could, was
the work of the artists who came to him to beg him
to sit for his picture or statue. Of the painters the
most eminent were Charles Peale and his son Rem-
brandt. Of the sculptors Houdon undoubtedly made
the best life-sized statue — that which still adorns
the Capitol at Richmond, Virginia — and from the
time it was first exhibited has been regarded as the
best, most lifelike. Another, sitting statue, was made
for the State of North Carolina by the Italian,
Canova, the most celebrated of the sculptors of that
day. The artist shows a Roman costume, a favorite
of his, unless, as in the case of Napoleon, he preferred
complete nudity. This statue was much injured in a
fire which nearly consumed the Capitol at Raleigh.
The English sculptor, Chantrey, executed a third
statue in which Washington was represented in mili-

THE "ATHENÆUM PORTRAIT"
By Gilbert Stuart

tary dress. This work used to be shown at the State House in Boston.

Of the many painted portraits of Washington, those by Gilbert Stuart have come to be accepted as authentic; especially the head in the painting which hung in the Boston Athenæum as a pendant to that of Martha Washington, and is now in the Boston Museum of Fine Arts. But as I remarked earlier, the fact that none of the painters indicate the very strong marks of smallpox (which he took on his trip to Barbados) on Washington's face creates a natural suspicion as to accuracy in detail of any of the portraits. Perhaps the divergence among them is not greater than that among those of Mary, Queen of Scots, and indicates only the marked incapacity of some of the painters who did them. We are certainly justified in saying that Washington's features varied considerably from his early prime to the days when he was President. We have come to talk about him as an old man because from the time when he was sixty years old he frequently used that expression himself; although, as he died at sixty-seven, he was never really "an old man." One wonders whether those who lived among pioneer conditions said and honestly believed that they were old at the time when, as we think, middle age would hardly have begun. Thus Abraham Lincoln writes of himself as a patri-

arch, and no doubt sincerely thought that he was, at a time when he had just reached forty. The two features in Washington's face about which the portraitists differ most are his nose and his mouth. In the early portrait by Charles Peale, his nose is slightly aquiline, but not at all so massive and conspicuous as in some of the later works. His mouth, and with it the expression of the lower part of his face, changed after he began to wear false teeth. Is it not fair to suppose that the effigies of Washington, made in later years and usually giving him a somewhat stiff and expansive grin, originated in the fact that his false set of teeth lacked perfect adjustment?

Thus Washington dropped into the ways of peace; working each day what would have been a long stint for a strong young man, and thinking, besides, more than most men thought of the needs and future of the country to which he had given liberty and independence. His chief anxiety henceforth was that the United States of America should not miss the great destiny for which he believed the Lord had prepared it.

CHAPTER VIII

WELDING THE NATION

THE doubt, the drifting, the incongruities and inconsistencies, the mistakes and follies which marked the five years after 1783 form what has been well called "The Critical Period of American History." They proved that the conquests of peace may not only be more difficult than the conquests of war, but that they may outlast those of war. Who should be the builders of the Ship of State? Those who had courage and clear vision, who loved justice, who were patient and humble and unflagging, and who believed with an ineluctable conviction that righteousness exalteth a nation; they were the simple fishermen who in the little church at Torcello predicted the splendor and power of Venice; they were the stern pioneers of Plymouth and Boston who laid the foundations of an empire greater than that of Rome.

It happened that during the American Revolution and immediately afterward, a larger number of such men existed in what had been the American Colonies than anywhere else at any other time in history. At the beginning of the Revolution, within a few weeks of the Declaration of Independence, some of these

men, impelled by a common instinct, adopted Articles of Confederation which should hold the former
Colonies together and enable them to maintain a
common front against the enemy during the war.
The Congress controlled military and civic affairs,
but the framers of the Articles were wary and too
timid to grant the Congress sufficient powers, with the
result that Washington, who embodied the dynamic
control of the war, was always most inadequately
supported; and as he fared, so fared his subordinates.

At the end of the war the Americans found that
they had won, not only freedom, but also Independence, the desire for which was not among their
original motives. Each of the thirteen States was
independent; they all felt the need of a union which
would enable them to protect themselves; of a common coinage and postage; of certain common laws
for criminal and similar cases; of a common government to direct their affairs with other nations. But
by habit and by training each was local rather than
National in its outlook. The Georgian had nothing
in common with the men of Massachusetts Bay
whose livelihood depended upon fisheries, or with the
Virginian of the Western border, to whom his relations
with the Indians were his paramount concern. The
Rhode Islander, busy with his manufactures, knew
and cared nothing for the South Carolinian with his

rice plantations. How to find a common denominator for all these? That was the business of them all.

The one thing which Washington regarded as likely and against which he wished to have every precaution taken, was a possible attempt of the English to pick a quarrel over some small matter and bring on a renewal of the war. Fortunately for the Americans, this did not happen. Washington knew our weakness so well that he could see how easy it would be for a bold and determined enemy to do us great if not fatal harm. But he did not know that the English themselves were in an almost desperate plight. By Rodney's decisive victory at sea they began to recover their ascendancy against the Coalition, but it was then too late to disavow the treaty. In Parliament George III had been defeated; the defeat meaning a very serious check to the policy which he had pursued for more than twenty years to fix royal tyranny on the British people. King George's system of personal government, himself being the person, had broken down and he could not revive it. Nearly seventy years were to elapse before Queen Victoria, who was as putty in the hands of her German husband, Prince Albert, rejoiced that he had restored the personal power of the British sovereign to a pitch it had not known since her grandfather George III.

The American Revolution had illustrated the fatal weakness of the Congress as an organ of government, and the Articles merely embodied the vagueness of the American people in regard to any real régime. The Congress has been much derided for its shortcomings and its blunders, although in truth not so much the Congress, as those who made it, was to blame. They had refused, in their timidity, to give it power to exercise control. It might not compel or enforce obedience. It did require General Washington during the war to furnish a regular report of his military actions and it put his suggestions on file where many of them grew yellow and dusty; but he might not strike, do that decisive act by which history is born. Their timidity made them see what he had accomplished not nearly so plainly as the dictator on horseback whom their fears conjured up.

During the war the sense of a common danger had lent the Congress a not easily defined but quite real coherence, which vanished when peace came, and the local ideals of the States took precedence. Take taxation. Congress could compute the quota of taxes which each State ought to pay, but it had no way of collecting or of enforcing payment. It took eighteen months to collect five per cent of the taxes laid in 1783. Of course a nation could not go on with such methods. No law binding all the States could be adopted unless every one of the thirteen States assented. Unanimity was almost unattainable; as when Governor Clinton of New York withheld his approval of a measure to improve a system of taxation to which the other twelve States had assented; so Rhode Island, the smallest of all, blocked another reform which twelve States had approved. Our foreign relations must be described as ignominious. Jefferson had taken Franklin's place as Minister to France, but we had no credit and he could not secure the loan he was seeking. John Adams in London, and John Jay in Madrid, were likewise balked. Jay had to submit to the closing of the lower Mississippi to American shipping. He did this in the hope of thereby conciliating Spain to make a commercial treaty which he thought was far more important than shipping. Our people in the Southwest, however, regarded the closing of the river as portending their ruin, and they threatened to secede if it were persisted in. Pennsylvania and New Jersey threw their weight with the Southerners and Congress voted against the Jay treaty. That was the time when the corsairs of the Barbary States preyed upon American shipping in the Mediterranean and seized crews of our vessels and sold them into slavery in Northern Africa. That there was not in the thirteen States sufficient feeling of dignity to resent and punish these outrages marks both their dispersed power and lack of regard for National honor.

After 1783 the States, virtually bankrupt at home, discordant, fickle, and aimless, and without credit or prestige abroad, were filled with many citizens who recognized that the system was bad and must be amended. The wise among them wrote treatises on the remedies they proposed. The wisest went to school of experience and sought in history how confederations and other political unions had fared. Washington wrote for his own use an account of the classical constitutions of Greece and Rome and of the more modern states; of the Amphictyonic Council among the ancient, and the Helvetic, Belgic, and Germanic among the more recent. John Adams devoted two massive volumes to an account of the medieval Italian republics. James Madison studied the Achaian League and other ancient combinations. There were many other men less eminent than these — there was a Peletiah Webster, for instance.

Washington viewed the situation as a pessimist. Was it because the high hopes that he had held during the war, that America should be the noblest among the nations, had been disappointed, or was it because he saw farther into the future than his colleagues saw? On May 18, 1786, he writes intimately to John Jay:

... We are certainly in a delicate situation; but my fear is that the people are not yet sufficiently *misled* to retract from error. To be plainer, I think there is more wickedness than ignorance mixed in our councils. Under this impression I scarcely know what opinion to entertain of a general convention. That it is necessary to revise and amend the Articles of Confederation, I entertain no doubt; but what may be the consequences of such an attempt is doubtful. Yet something must be done, or the fabric must fall, for it certainly is tottering.

Ignorance and design are difficult to combat. Out of these proceed illiberal sentiments, improper jealousies, and a train of evils which oftentimes in republican governments must be sorely felt before they can be removed. The former, that is ignorance, being a fit soil for the latter to work in, tools are employed by them which a generous mind would disdain to use; and which nothing but time, and their own puerile or wicked productions, can show the inefficacy and dangerous tendency of. I think often of our situation, and view it with concern. From the high ground we stood upon, from the plain path which invited our footsteps, to be so fallen! so lost! it is really mortifying.[1]

One of the chief causes of the discontents which troubled the public was the increasing number of persons who had been made debtors after the war by the more and more pressing demands of their creditors. These debtors knew nothing about economics; they only knew that they were being crushed by persons more lucky than themselves. In Massachusetts they broke out in actual rebellion named

[1] Ford, XI, 31.

after the man who led it, Daniel Shays. They were put down by the more or less doubtful appeal to veterans of the National Army, but their ebullition was not forgotten as a symptom of a very dangerous condition. In 1786 representatives from five States met in a convention at Annapolis to consider the hard times and the troubles in trade. Washington, Hamilton, and Madison were thought to be behind the convention, which accomplished little, but made it clear that a large general convention ought to meet and to discuss the way of securing a strong central government. This convention was discussed during that summer and autumn, and a call was issued for a meeting in the following spring at Philadelphia. Virginia turned first to Washington to be one of its delegates, but he had sincere scruples against entering public life again. He wrote to James Madison on November 18th:

Although I had bid adieu to the public walks of life in a public manner, and had resolved never more to tread upon public ground, yet if, upon an occasion so interesting to the well-being of the confederacy, it should have appeared to have been the wish of the Assembly to have employed me with other associates in the business of revising the federal system, I should, from a sense of obligation I am under for repeated proof of confidence in me, more than from any opinion I should have entertained of my usefulness, have obeyed its call; but it is now out of my power to do so with any degree of consistency.[1]

[1] Ford, XI, 87.

Washington's disinclination to abandon the quiet of Mount Vernon and the congenial work he found there, and to be plunged again into political labors, was perhaps his strongest reason for making this decision. But a temporary aggravation ruled him. The Society of the Cincinnati, of which he was president, had aroused much odium in the country among those who were jealous or envious that such a special privileged class should exist, and among those who really believed that it had the secret design of establishing an aristocracy if not actually a monarchy. Washington held that its original avowed purpose, to keep the officers who had served in the Revolution together, would perpetuate the patriotic spirit which enabled them to win, and might be a source of strength in case of further ordeals. But when he found that public sentiment ran so strongly against the Cincinnati, he withdrew as its president and he told Madison that he would vote to have the Society disbanded if it were not that it counted a minority of foreign members. Stronger than a desire for a private life and for the ease of Mount Vernon was his sense of duty as a patriot; so that when this was strongly urged upon him he gave way and consented.

Spring came, the snows melted in the Northern States, and through the month of April the delegates to this Convention started from their homes in the North and in the South for Philadelphia. The first regular session was held on May 25th, although some of the delegates did not arrive until several weeks later. They sat in Independence Hall in the same room where, eleven years before, the Declaration of Independence had been adopted and signed. Of the members in the new Convention, George Washington was easily the first. His commanding figure, tall and straight and in no wise impaired by eight years' campaigns and hardships, was almost the first to attract the attention of any one who looked upon that assembly. He was fifty-five years old. Next in reputation was the patriarch, Benjamin Franklin, twenty-seven years his senior, shrewd, wise, poised, tart, good-natured; whose prestige was thought to be sufficient to make him a worthy presiding officer when Washington was not present. James Madison of Virginia was among the young men of the Convention, being only thirty-six years old, and yet almost at the top of them all in constitutional learning. More precocious still was Alexander Hamilton of New York, who was only thirty, one of the most remarkable examples of a statesman who developed very early and whom Death cut off before he showed any signs of a decline. One figure we miss — that of Thomas Jefferson of Virginia, tall and wiry and red-curled, who was absent in Paris as Minister to France.

Massachusetts sent four representatives, important but not preëminent — Elbridge Gerry, Nathaniel Gorham, Rufus King, and Caleb Strong. New York had only two besides Hamilton; Robert Yates and John Lansing. Pennsylvania trusted most to Benjamin Franklin, but she sent the financier of the Revolution, Robert Morris, and Gouverneur Morris; and with them went Thomas Mifflin, George Clymer, Thomas Fitzsimmons, Jared Ingersoll, James Wilson — all conspicuous public men at the time, although their fame is bedraggled or quite faded now. Wilson ranked as the first lawyer of the group. Of the five from little Delaware sturdy John Dickinson, a man who thought, was no negligible quantity.

Connecticut also had as spokesmen two strong individualities — Roger Sherman and Oliver Ellsworth. Maryland spoke through James McHenry and Daniel Carroll and three others of greater obscurity. Virginia had George Washington, President of the Convention, and James Madison, active, resourceful, and really accomplishing; and in addition to these two: Edmund Randolph, the Governor; George Mason, Washington's hard-headed and discreet lawyer friend; John Blair, George Wythe, and

James McClurg. From South Carolina went three unusual orators, John Rutledge, C. C. Pinckney and Charles Pinckney, and Pierce Butler. Georgia named four mediocre but useful men.

In this gathering of fifty-five persons, the proportion between those who were preëminent for common sense and those who were remarkable for special knowledge and talents was very fairly kept. Most of them had had experience in dealing with men either in local government offices or in the army. Socially, they came almost without exception from respectable if not aristocratic families. Of the fifty-five, twenty-nine were university or college bred, their universities comprising Oxford, Glasgow, and Edinburgh besides the American Harvard, William and Mary, Yale, Princeton, and Columbia. The two foremost members, Washington and Franklin, were not college bred. Among the fifty-five we do not find John Adams and Thomas Jefferson, who, as I have said, were in Europe on official business. John Jay also was lacking, because, as it appears, the Anti-Federalists did not wish him to represent them in the Convention; but his influence permeated it and the wider public, who later read his unsigned articles in "The Federalist." Samuel Adams, Patrick Henry, and Richard Henry Lee stayed at home. General Nathanael Greene, the favorite son of Rhode Island, would have been at the Convention but for his untimely death a few weeks before the preceding Christmas.

Owing to delays the active business of the Convention halted, although for at least a fortnight the members who had come promptly carried on unofficial discussions. Washington, being chosen President without a competitor, presided, with perhaps more than his habitual gravity and punctilio. The members took their work very seriously. The debates lasted five or six hours a day, and, as they were continued consecutively until the autumn, there was ample time to discuss many subjects. The Convention adopted strict secrecy as its rule, so that its proceedings were not known by the public nor was any satisfactory report of them kept and published. At the time there was objection to this provision, and now, after more than a century and a third, we must regret that we can never know many points in regard to the actual give and take of discussion in this the most fateful of all assemblies. But from Madison's memoranda and reminiscences we can infer a good deal as to what went on.

The wisdom of keeping the proceedings secret was fully justified. The framers of the Constitution knew that it was to a large degree a new experiment, that it would be subjected to all kinds of criticism, but that it must be judged by its entirety and not by its parts; and that therefore it must be presented entire. At the outset some of the members, foreseeing opposition, were for suggesting palliatives and for sugar-coating. Some of the measures they feared might excite hostility. To these suggestions Washington made a brief but very noble remonstrance which seemed deeply to impress his hearers. And no one could question that it gave the keynote on which he hoped to maintain the business of the Convention. "It is too probable that no plan we propose will be adopted," Washington said very gravely. "Perhaps another dreadful conflict is to be sustained. If, to please the people, we offer what we ourselves disapprove, how can we afterward defend our work? Let us raise a standard to which the wise and honest can repair; the event is in the hand of God."[1] Among the obstacles which seemed very serious—and many believed they would wreck the Convention—was the question of slavery. By this time all the northern part of the country favored its abolition. Even Virginia was on that side. For practical planters like George Washington knew that it was the most costly and least productive form of labor. They opposed it on economic rather than moral grounds. Farther South, however, especially in

[1] Fiske, *Critical Period*, 250.

South Carolina where the negroes seemed to be the only kind of laborers for the rice-fields, and in those regions where they harvested the cotton, the whites insisted that slavery should be maintained. The contest seemed likely to be very fierce between the disputants, and then, with true Anglo-Saxon instinct, they sought for a compromise. The South had regarded slaves as chattels. The compromise brought forward by Madison consisted in agreeing that five slaves should count in population as three. By this curious device a negro was equivalent to three fifths of a white man. Such a compromise was, of course, illogical, leaving the question whether negroes were chattels or human beings with even a theoretical civil character undecided. But many of the members, who saw the illogic quite plainly, voted for it, being dazzled if not seduced by the thought that it was a compromise which would stave off an irreconcilable conflict at least for the present; so Washington, who wished the abolition of slavery, voted for the compromise along with Charles Cotesworth Pinckney, the South Carolinian who regarded slavery as higher than any of the Ten Commandments.

The second compromise referred to the slave trade, which was particularly defended by South Carolina and Georgia. The raising of rice and indigo in those States caused an increasing death-rate among the slaves. The slave trade, which brought many kidnapped slaves from Africa to those States was needed to replenish the number of slaves who died. Virginia had not yet become an important breeding-place of slaves who were sold to planters farther south. The members of the Convention who wished to put an end to this hideous traffic proposed that it should be prohibited, and that the enforcement of the prohibition should be assigned to the General Government. Pinckney, however, keen to defend his privileged institution and the special interests of his State, bluntly informed the Convention that if they voted to abolish the slave trade, South Carolina would regard it as a polite way of telling her that she was not wanted in the new Union. To think of attempting to form a Union without South Carolina amazed them all and made them pliable. Although there was considerable opposition to giving the General Government control over shipping, this provision was passed. The Northerners saw in it the germs of a tariff act which would benefit their manufacturers, and they agreed that the slave trade should not be interfered with before 1808 and that no export tax should be authorized.

The third compromise affected representation. The Convention had already voted that the Congress should consist of two parts, a Senate and a House of Representatives. By a really clever device each State sent two members to the Senate, thus equalizing the small and large States in that branch of the Government. The House, on the other hand, represented the People, and the number of members elected from each State corresponded, therefore, to the population.

As I do not attempt to make even a summary of the details of the Convention, I should pass over many of the other topics which it considered, often with very heated discussion. The fundamental problem was how to preserve the rights of the States and at the same time give the Central Government sufficient power. By devices which actually worked, and for many years continued to work, this conflict was smoothed over, although sixty years later the question of State rights, intertwined with that of slavery, nearly split the Nation in the War of Secession. There was much question as to the term for which the President should be elected and whether by the People or by Congress. Some were for one, two, three, four, ten, and even fifteen years. Rufus King, grown sarcastic, said: "Better call it twenty — it's the average reign of princes." Alexander Hamilton and Gouverneur Morris stood for a life service with provision for the President's removal in case of mal-

feasance. These gentlemen, in spite of their influence
in the Convention, stirred up a deep-seated enmity
to their plan. Few instincts were more general than
that which drew back from any arrangement which
might embolden the monarchists to make a man
President for a ten or fifteen years' term or for life.
This could not fail to encourage those who wished
for the equivalent of an hereditary prince. The Convention soon made it evident that they would have
none but a short term, and they chose, finally, four
years. There was a debate over the question of his
election; should he be chosen directly by the legislature, or by electors? The strong men — Mason,
Rutledge, Roger Sherman, and Strong — favored
the former; stronger men — Washington, Madison,
Gerry, and Gouverneur Morris — favored the latter,
and it prevailed. Nevertheless, the Electoral College
thus created soon became, and has remained, as useless as a vermiform appendix.

Towards the end of the summer the Convention
had completed its first draft of the Constitution;
then they handed their work over to a Committee for
Style and Arrangement, composed of W. S. Johnson
of North Carolina, Hamilton, Gouverneur Morris,
Madison, and King. Then, on September 17th, the
Constitution of the United States was formally published. This document, done "by the Unanimous

Consent of the States present," was sent to the Governor or Legislature of each State with the understanding that its ratification by nine States would be required before it was proclaimed the law of the land.

In his diary for Monday, the seventeenth of September, 1787, Washington makes this entry:

> Met in Convention, when the Constitution received the unanimous consent of 11 States and Colo. Hamilton's from New York [the only delegate from thence in Convention], and was subscribed to by every member present, except Governor Randolph and Colo. Mason from Virginia, & Mr. Gerry from Massachusetts.
> The business being thus closed, the members adjourned to the City Tavern, dined together, and took a cordial leave of each other. After which I returned to my lodgings, did some business with, and received the papers from the Secretary of the Convention, and retired to meditate on the momentous wk. which had been executed, after not less than five, for a large part of the time six and sometimes 7 hours sitting every day, [except] Sundays & the ten days adjournment to give a Comee. [Committee] opportunity & time to arrange the business for more than four months.[1]

One likes to think of Washington presiding over that Convention for more than four months, seeing one suggestion after another brought forward and debated until finally disposed of, he saying little except to enforce the rules of parliamentary

[1] Ford, XI, 155.

debate. No doubt his asides (and part of his conversation) frankly gave his opinion as to each measure, because he never disguised his thoughts and he seems to have voted when the ballots were taken — a practice unusual to modern presiding officers except in case of a tie. His summing-up of the Constitution, which he wrote on the day after the adjournment in a hurried letter to Lafayette, is given briefly in these lines:

It is the result of four months' deliberation. It is now a child of fortune, to be fostered by some and buffeted by others. What will be the general opinion, or the reception of it, is not for me to decide; nor shall I say anything for or against it. If it be good, I suppose it will work its way; if bad, it will recoil on the framers.

A month later, in the seclusion of Mount Vernon, he spread the same news before his friend General Knox:

... The Constitution is now before the judgment-seat. It has, as was expected, its adversaries and supporters. Which will preponderate is yet to be decided. The former more than probably will be most active, as the major part of them will, it is to be feared, be governed by sinister and self-important motives, to which everything in their breasts must yield. ...

The other class, he said, would probably ask itself whether the Constitution now submitted was not better than the inadequate and precarious government under which they had been living. If there

were defects, as doubtless there were, did it not provide means for amending them? Then he concludes
with a gleam of optimism:

... Is it not likely that real defects will be as readily
discovered after as before trial? and will not our successors be as ready to apply the remedy as ourselves, if
occasion should require it? To think otherwise will, in
my judgment, be ascribing more of the amor patriæ,
more wisdom and more virtue to ourselves, than I
think we deserve.[1]

Nearly five months later, February 7, 1788, he
wrote Lafayette what we may consider a more deliberate opinion:

As to my sentiments with respect to the merits of the
new constitution, I will disclose them without reserve,
(although by passing through the post-office they should
become known to all the world,) for in truth I have
nothing to conceal on that subject. It appears to me,
then, little short of a miracle, that the delegates from so
many different States (which States you know are also
different from each other), in their manners, circumstances, and prejudices, should unite in forming a system of national government, so little liable to well-
founded objections. Nor am I yet such an enthusiastic,
partial, or indiscriminating admirer of it, as not to perceive it is tinctured with some real (though not radical)
defects. The limits of a letter would not suffer me to go
fully into an examination of them; nor would the discussion be entertaining or profitable. I therefore for-
bear to touch upon it. With regard to the two great
points (the pivots upon which the whole machine must
move), my creed is simply,

[1] Ford, XI, 173.

1st. That the general government is not invested with more powers, than are indispensably necessary to perfrom the functions of a good government; and consequently, that no objection ought to be made against the quantity of power delegated to it.

2nd. That these powers (as the appointment of all rulers will for ever arise from, and at short, stated intervals recur to, the free suffrage of the people), are so distributed among the legislative, executive, and judicial branches, into which the general government is arranged, that it can never be in danger of degenerating into a monarchy, an oligarchy, an aristocracy, or any other despotic or oppressive form, so long as there shall remain any virtue in the body of the people.

I would not be understood, my dear Marquis, to speak of consequences, which may be produced in the revolution of ages, by corruption of morals, profligacy of manners and listlessness for the preservation of the natural and unalienable rights of mankind, nor of the successful usurpations, that may be established at such an unpropitious juncture upon the ruins of liberty, however providently guarded and secured; as these are contingencies against which no human prudence can effectually provide. It will at least be a recommendation to the proposed constitution, that it is provided with more checks and barriers against the introduction of tyranny, and those of a nature less liable to be surmounted, than any government hitherto instituted among mortals hath possessed. We are not to expect perfection in this world; but mankind, in modern times, have apparently made some progress in the science of government. Should that which is now offered to the people of America, be found on experiment less perfect than it can be made, a constitutional door is left open for its amelioration.[1]

[1] Ford, XI, 218-21.

Thus was accomplished the American Constitution. Gladstone has said of it in well-known words
that, just "as the British Constitution is the most
subtle organism which has proceeded from the womb
and the long gestation of progressive history, so the
American Constitution is so far as I can see the most
wonderful work ever struck off at a given time by
the brain and purpose of man." [1] Note that Gladstone does not name a single or an individual man,
which would have been wholly untrue, for the American Constitution was struck off by the wisdom and
foresight of fifty-five men collectively. There were
among them two or three who might be called tran-
scendent men. It gained its peculiar value from the
fact that it represents the composite of many diver-
gent opinions and different characters.

Just before the members broke up at their final
meeting in Independence Hall, Benjamin Franklin
amused them with a characteristic bit of raillery.
On the back of the President's black chair, a half sun
was carved and emblazoned. "During all these
weeks," said Franklin, "I have often wondered
whether that sun was rising or setting. I know now
that it is a rising sun."

The first State to ratify the Constitution was
Delaware, on December 6, 1787. Pennsylvania fol-

[1] W. E. Gladstone, *North American Review*, September, 1878.

lowed on December 12th, and New Jersey on December 18th. Ratifications continued without haste until New Hampshire, the ninth State, signed on June 21, 1788. Four days later, Virginia, a very important State, ratified. New York, which had been Anti-Federalist throughout, joined the majority on July 26th. North Carolina waited until November 21st, and little Rhode Island, the last State of all, did not come in until May 29, 1790. But, as the adherence of nine States sufficed, the affirmative action of New Hampshire on June 21, 1788, constituted the legal beginning of the United States of America.

No test could be more winnowing than that to which the Constitution was subjected during more than eighteen months before its adoption. In each State, in each section, its friends and enemies discussed it at meetings and in private gatherings. In New York, for instance, it was only the persistence of Alexander Hamilton and his unfailing oratory, unmatched until then in this country, that routed the Anti-Federalists at Poughkeepsie and caused the victory of the Federalists in the State. In Virginia, Patrick Henry, who had said on the eve of the Revolution, "I am not a Virginian, but an American," still held out. Nevertheless, the more the people of the country discussed the matter, the surer was their conviction that Washington was right when he intimated that they must prefer the new Constitution unless they could show reason for supposing that the anarchy towards which the old order was swiftly driving them was preferable.

During the autumn of 1788 peaceful electioneering went on throughout the country. Among the last acts of that thin wraith, the Continental Congress, was a decree that Presidential Electors should be chosen on the first Wednesday of January, 1789; that they should vote for President on the first Wednesday in February, and that the new Congress should meet on the first Wednesday in March. The State of New York, where Anti-Federalists swarmed, did not follow the decree — with the result that that State, which had been behindhand in signing the Declaration of Independence, failed through the intrigues of the Anti-Federalists to choose electors, and so had no part in the choice of Washington as President of the United States. The other ten States performed their duty on time. They elected Washington President by a unanimous vote of sixty-nine out of sixty-nine votes cast.

The Vice-Presidential contest was perplexing, there being many candidates who received only a few votes each. Many persons thought that it would be fitting that Samuel Adams, the father of the Revolution, should be chosen to serve with Washington,

the father of his country; but too many remembered
that he had been hostile to the Federalists until almost the end of the preliminary canvass and so they
did not think that he ought to be chosen. The successful man was John Adams, who had been a robust
Patriot from the beginning and had served honor-
ably and devotedly in every position which he had
held since 1775.

On April 14th Washington's election was notified
to him, and on the 16th he bade farewell to Mount
Vernon, where he had hoped to pass the rest of his
days in peace and home duties and agriculture, and
he rode in what proved to be a triumphal march to
New York. That city was chosen the capital of the
new Nation. Streams of enthusiastic and joyous
citizens met and acclaimed him at every town
through which he passed. At Trenton a party of
thirteen young girls decked out in muslin and
wreaths represented the thirteen States, and perhaps brought to his mind the contrast between that
day and thirteen years before when he crossed the
Delaware on boats amid floating cakes of ice and the
pelting of sleet and rain. On April 23d he entered
New York City. A week later at noon a military
escort attended him from his lodging to Federal Hall
at the corner of Wall and Nassau Streets, where a
vast crowd awaited him. Washington stood on a

balcony. All could witness the ceremony. The Secretary of the Senate bore a Bible upon a velvet cushion, and Chancellor Livingston administered the oath of office. Washington's head was still bowed when Livingston shouted: "Long live George Washington, President of the United States!" The crowds took up the cheer, which spread to many parts of the city and was repeated in all parts of the United States.

CHAPTER IX

THE FIRST AMERICAN PRESIDENT

THE inauguration of Washington on April 30, 1789, brought a new type of administration into the world. The democracy which it initiated was very different from that of antiquity, from the models of Greece and of Rome, and quite different from that of the Italian republics during the Middle Age. The head of the new State differed essentially from the monarchs across the sea. Although there were varieties of traditions and customs in what had been the Colonies, still their dominant characteristic was British. According to the social traditions of Virginia, George Washington was an aristocrat, but in contrast with the British, he was a democrat.

He believed, however, that the President must guard his office from the free-and-easy want of decorum which some of his countrymen regarded as the stamp of democracy. At his receptions he wore a black velvet suit with gold buckles at the knee and on his shoes, and yellow gloves, and profusely powdered hair carried in a silk bag behind. In one hand he held a cocked hat with an ostrich plume; on his left thigh he wore a sword in a white scabbard of polished leather. He shook hands with no one; but acknowledged the courtesy of his visitors by a very formal bow. When he drove, it was in a coach with four or six handsome horses and outriders and lackeys dressed in resplendent livery.

After his inauguration he spoke his address to the Congress, and several days later members of the House and of the Senate called on him at his residence and made formal replies to his Inaugural Address. After a few weeks, experience led him to modify somewhat his daily schedule. He found that unless it was checked, the insatiate public would consume all his time. Every Tuesday afternoon, between three and four o'clock, he had a public reception which any one might attend. Likewise, on Friday afternoons, Mrs. Washington had receptions of her own. The President accepted no invitations to dinner, but at his own table there was an unending succession of invited guests, except on Sunday, which he observed privately. Interviews with the President could be had at any time that suited his convenience. Thus did he arrange to transact his regular or his private business.

Inevitably, some of the public objected to his rules and pretended to see very strong monarchical leanings in them. But the country took them as he intended, and there can be no doubt that it felt the benefit of his promoting the dignity of his office. Equally beneficial was his rule of not appointing to any office any man merely because he was the President's friend. Washington knew that such a consideration would give the candidate an unfair advantage. He knew further that office-holders who could screen themselves behind the plea that they were the President's friends might be very embarrassing to him. As office-seekers became, with the development of the Republic, among the most pernicious of its evils and of its infamies, we can but feel grateful that so far as in him lay Washington tried to keep them within bounds.

In all his official acts he took great pains not to force his personal wishes. He knew that both in prestige and popularity he held a place apart among his countrymen, and for this reason he did not wish to have measures passed simply because they were his. Accordingly, in the matter of receiving the public and in granting interviews and of ceremonials at the Presidential Residence, he asked the advice of John Adams, John Jay, Hamilton, and Jefferson, and he listened to many of their suggestions. Colonel Humphreys, who had been one of his aides-de-camp and was staying in the Presidential Residence, acted as Chamberlain at the first reception. Humphreys took an almost childish delight in gold braid and flummery. At a given moment the door of the large hall in which the concourse of guests was assembled was opened and he, advancing, shouted, with a loud voice: "The President of the United States!" Washington followed him and went through the paces prescribed by the Colonel with punctilious exactness, but with evident lack of relish. When the levee broke up and the party had gone, Washington said to Colonel Humphreys: "Well, you have taken me in once, but, by God, you shall never take me in a second time."[1] Irving, who borrows this story from Jefferson, warns us that perhaps Jefferson was not a credible witness.

Congress transacted much important business at this first session. It determined that the President should have a Cabinet of men whose business it was to administer the chief departments and to advise the President. Next in importance were the financial measures proposed by the Secretary of the Treasury. Washington chose for his first Cabinet Ministers: Thomas Jefferson, who had not returned from Paris, as Secretary of State, or Foreign Minister as he was first called; Alexander Hamilton, Secretary of the Treasury; General Henry Knox, Secretary of War; and Edmund Randolph, Attorney-General. Of these, Hamilton had to face the most

[1] Irving, v, 14.

bitter opposition. Throughout the Revolution the former Colonies had never been able to collect enough money to pay the expense of the war and the other charges of the Confederation. The Confederation handed over a considerable debt to the new Government. Besides this many of the States had paid each its own cost of equipping and maintaining its contingent. Hamilton now proposed that the United States Government should assume these various State debts, which would aggregate $21,000,000 and bring the National debt to a total of $75,000,000. Hamilton's suggestion that the State debts be assumed caused a vehement outcry. Its opponents protested that no fair adjustment could be reached. The Assumptionists retorted that this would be the only fair settlement, but the Anti-Assumptionists voted them down by a majority of two. In other respects, Hamilton's financial measures prospered, and before many months he seized the opportunity of making a bargain by which the next Congress reversed its vote on Assumption. In less than a year the members of Congress and many of the public had reached the conclusion that New York City was not the best place to be the capital of the Nation. The men from the South argued that it put the South to a disadvantage, as its ease of access to New York, New Jersey, and the Eastern States gave that sec-

tion of the country a too favorable situation. There
was a strong party in favor of Philadelphia, but it
was remembered that in the days of the Confederation a gang of turbulent soldiers had dashed down
from Lancaster and put to flight the Convention sitting at Philadelphia. Nevertheless, Philadelphia was
chosen temporarily, the ultimate choice of a situation
being farther south on the Potomac.

Jefferson returned from France in the early winter. The discussion over Assumption was going on
very virulently. It happened that one day Jefferson
met Hamilton, and this is his account of what
followed:

As I was going to the President's one day, I met him
[Hamilton] in the street. He walked me backwards and
forwards before the President's door for half an hour.
He painted pathetically the temper into which the legislature had been wrought; the disgust of those who
were called the creditor States; the danger of the secession of their members, and the separation of the States.
He observed that the members of the administration
ought to act in concert; that though this question was
not of my department, yet a common duty should make
it a common concern; that the President was the centre
on which all administrative questions ultimately rested,
and that all of us should rally around him and support,
with joint efforts, measures approved by him; and that
the question having been lost by a small majority only,
it was probable that an appeal from me to the judgment
and discretion of some of my friends, might effect a
change in the vote, and the machine of government,

now suspended, might be again set into motion. I told him that I was really a stranger to the whole subject, that not having yet informed myself of the system of finance adopted, I knew not how far this was a necessary sequence; that undoubtedly, if its rejection endangered a dissolution of our Union at this incipient stage, I should deem it most unfortunate of all consequences to avert which all partial and temporary evils should be yielded. I proposed to him, however, to dine with me the next day, and I would invite another friend or two, bring them into conference together, and I thought it impossible that reasonable men, consulting together coolly, could fail, by some mutual sacrifices of opinion, to form a compromise which was to save the Union. The discussion took place. I could take no part in it but an exhortatory one, because I was a stranger to the circumstances which should govern it. But it was finally agreed, that whatever importance had been attached to the rejection of this proposition, the preservation of the Union and of concord among the States was more important, and that, therefore, it would be better that the vote of rejection should be rescinded, to effect which some members should change their votes. But it was observed that this pill would be peculiarly bitter to the Southern States, and that some concomitant measure should be adopted to sweeten it a little to them. There had before been projects to fix the seat of government either at Philadelphia or at Georgetown on the Potomac; and it was thought that, by giving it to Philadelphia for ten years, and to Georgetown permanently afterwards, this might, as an anodyne, solve in some degree the ferment which might be excited by the other measure alone. So two of the Potomac members (White and Lee, but White with a revulsion of stomach almost convulsive) agreed to change their votes, and Hamilton undertook to carry the other point. In doing this, the influence he had established over the eastern members, with the agency of Robert Morris with those of the Middle States, effected his side of the engagement.[1]

As a result of Hamilton's bargain, the bill for Assumption was passed, and it was agreed that Philadelphia should be the capital for ten years and that afterwards a new city should be built on the banks of the Potomac and made the capital permanently.

During the summer of 1789 Washington suffered the most serious sickness of his entire life. The cause was anthrax in his thigh, and at times it seemed that it would prove fatal. For many weeks he was forced to lie on one side, with frequent paroxysms of great pain. After a month and a half he began to mend, but very slowly, so that autumn came before he got up and could go about again. His medical adviser was Dr. Samuel Bard of New York, and Irving reports the following characteristic conversation between him and his patient: "Do not flatter me with vain hopes," said Washington, with placid firmness; "I am not afraid to die, and therefore can bear the worst." The doctor expressed hope, but owned that he had apprehensions. "Whether to-night or twenty years hence, makes no difference," observed Wash-

[1] *Jefferson's Works*, IX, 93.

ington. "I know that I am in the hands of a good
Providence." [1] His friends thought that he never
really recovered his old-time vigor. That autumn,
as soon as Congress had adjourned, he took a journey through New England, going as far as Portsmouth and returning in time for the opening of the
Second Congress.

The Government was now settling down into what
became its normal routine. The Cabinet was completed by the appointment of Jefferson as Secretary of State and Edmund Randolph as Attorney-
General. Jefferson would have preferred to go back
to France as American Minister, but in a fulsome
letter he declared himself willing to accept any
office which Washington wished him to fill. The
Supreme Court was organized with John Jay as
Chief Justice, and five Associate Justices. Washington could not fail to be aware that parties were beginning to shape themselves. At first the natural
divisions consisted of the Federalists, who believed
in adopting the Constitution, and those who did not.
As soon as the thirteen States voted to accept the
Constitution, the Anti-Federalists had no definite
motive for existing. Their place was taken principally by the Republicans over against whom were
the Democrats. A few years later these parties ex-

[1] Irving, v, 22.

changed names. A fundamental difference in the ideas of the Americans sprang from their views in regard to National and State rights. Some of them regarded the State as the ultimate unit. Others insisted that the Nation was sovereign. These two conflicting views run through American history down to the Civil War, and even in Washington's time they existed in outline. Washington himself was a Federalist, believing that the Federation of the former Colonies should be made as compact and strongly knit as possible. He had had too much evidence during the Revolution of the weakness of uncentralized government, and yet his Virginia origin and training had planted in him a strong sympathy for State rights. In Washington's own Cabinet dwelt side by side the leaders of the two parties: Thomas Jefferson, the Secretary of State, though born in Virginia of high aristocratic stock, was the most aggressive and infatuated of Democrats. Alexander Hamilton, born in the West Indies and owing nothing to family connections, was a natural aristocrat. He believed that the educated and competent few must inevitably govern the incompetent masses. His enemies suspected that he leaned strongly towards monarchy and would have been glad to see Washington crowned king.

President Washington, believing in Assumption,

took satisfaction in Hamilton's bargain with Jefferson which made Assumption possible. For the President saw in the act a power making for union, and union was one of the chief objects of his concern. The foremost of Hamilton's measures, however, for good or for ill, was the protective tariff on foreign imports. Experience has shown that protection has been much more than a financial device. It has been deeply and inextricably moral. It has caused many American citizens to seek for tariff favors from the Government. Compared with later rates, those which Hamilton's tariff set were moderate indeed. The highest duties it exacted on foreign imports were fifteen per cent, while the average was only eight and a half per cent. And yet it had not been long in force when the Government was receiving $200,000 a month, which enabled it to defray all the necessary public charges. Hamilton, in the words of Daniel Webster, "smote the rock of National resources and copious streams of wealth poured forth. He touched the dead corpse of public credit and it stood forth erect with life." The United States of all modern countries have been the best fitted by their natural resources to do without artificial stimulation, in spite of which fact they still cling, after one hundred and thirty-five years, to the easy and plausible tariff makeshift. Washington himself believed that the tariff should so promote industries as to provide for whatever the country needed in time of war.

Two other financial measures are to be credited to Hamilton. The first was the excise, an internal revenue on distilled spirits. It met with opposition from the advocates of State rights, but was passed after heated debate. The last was the establishment of a United States Bank. All of Hamilton's measures tended directly to centralization, the object which he and Washington regarded as paramount.

In 1790 Washington made a second trip through the Eastern States, taking pains to visit Rhode Island, which was the last State to ratify the Constitution (May 29, 1790). These trips of his, for which the hostile might have found parallels in the royal progresses of the British sovereigns, really served a good purpose; for they enabled the people to see and hear their President; which had a good effect in a newly established nation. Washington lost no opportunity for teaching a moral. Thus, when he came to Boston, John Hancock, the Governor of Massachusetts, seemed to wish to indicate that the Governor was the highest personage in the State and not at all subservient even to the President of the United States. He wished to arrange it so that Washington should call on him first, but this Wash-

ington had no idea of doing. Hancock then wrote
and apologized for not greeting the President owing
to an unfortunate indisposition. Washington replied
regretting the Governor's illness and announcing
that the schedule on which he was travelling required
him to quit Boston at a given time. Governor Hancock, whose spectacular signature had given him
prominence everywhere, finding that he could not
make the President budge, sent word that he was
coming to pay his respects. Washington replied that
he should be much pleased to welcome him, but
expressed anxiety lest the Governor might increase
his indisposition by coming out. This little comedy
had a far-reaching effect. It settled the question as
to whether the Governor of a State or the President
of the United States should take precedence. From
that day to this, no Governor, so far as I am aware,
has set himself above the President in matters of
ceremonial.

One of the earliest difficulties which Washington's
administration had to overcome was the hostility of
the Indians. Indian discontent and even lawlessness
had been going on for years, with only a desultory
and ineffectual show of vigor on the part of the
whites. Washington, who detested whatever was
ineffectual and lacking in purpose, determined to
beat down the Indians into submission. He sent out a

THE " GOODHUE PORTRAIT " OF WASHINGTON
1790

first army under General St. Clair, but it was taken in ambush by the Indians and nearly wiped out — a disaster which caused almost a panic throughout the Western country. Washington felt the losses deeply, but he had no intention of being beaten there. He organized a second army, gave it to General Wayne to command, who finally brought the Six Nations to terms. The Indians in the South still remained unpacified and lawless.

Washington made another prolonged trip, this time through the Southern States, which greatly improved his health and gave an opportunity of seeing many of the public men, and enabled the population to greet for the first time their President. Meanwhile the seeds of partisan feuds grew apace, as they could not fail to do where two of the ablest politicians ever known in the United States sat in the same Cabinet and pursued with unremitting energy ideas that were mutually uncompromising. Thomas Jefferson, although born of the old aristocratic stock of Virginia, had early announced himself a Democrat, and had led that faction throughout the Revolution. His facile and fiery mind gave to the Declaration of Independence an irresistible appeal, and it still remains after nearly one hundred and fifty years one of the most contagious documents ever drawn up. Going to France at the outbreak of

the French Revolution, he found the French nation
about to put into practice the principles on which he
had long fed his imagination — principles which he
accepted without qualification and without scruple.
Returning to America after the organization of the
Government, he accepted with evident reluctance
the position of Secretary of State which Washington
offered to him. In the Cabinet his chief adversary
or competitor was Alexander Hamilton, his junior
by fourteen years, a man equally versatile and
equally facile — and still more enthralling as an
orator. Hamilton harbored the anxiety that the
United States under their new Constitution would
be too loosely held together. He promoted, therefore,
every measure that tended to strengthen the Central Government and to save it from dissolution
either by the collapse of its unifying bonds or by anarchy. In the work of the first two years of Washington's administration, Hamilton was plainly victorious. The Tariff Law, the Excise, the National
Bank, the National Funding Bill, all centraliz-
ing measures, were his. Washington approved them
all, and we may believe that he talked them over
with Hamilton and gave them his approval before
they came under public discussion.

Thus, as Hamilton gained, Jefferson plainly lost.
But Washington did not abandon his sound position

as a neutral between the two. He requested Jefferson and Edmund Randolph to draw up objections to some of Hamilton's schemes, so that he had in writing the arguments of very strong opponents.

Meanwhile the French Revolution had broken all bounds, and Jefferson, as the sponsor of the French over here, was kept busy in explaining and defending the Gallic horrors. The Americans were in a large sense law-abiding, but in another sense they were lawless. Nevertheless, they heard with horror of the atrocities of the French Revolutionists — of the drownings, of the guillotining, of the imprisonment and execution of the King and Queen — and they had a healthy distrust of the Jacobin Party, which boasted that these things were natural accompaniments of Liberty with which they planned to conquer the world. Events in France inevitably drove that country into war with England. Washington and his chief advisers believed that the United States ought to remain neutral as between the two belligerents. But neutrality was difficult. In spite of their horror at the French Revolution, the memory of our debt to France during our own Revolution made a very strong bond of sympathy, whereas our long record of hostility to England during our Colony days, and since the Declaration of Independence, kept alive a traditional hatred for Great Britain. While it was easy, therefore, to preach neutrality, it was very difficult to enforce it. An occurrence which could not have been foreseen further added to the difficulty of neutrality.

In the spring of 1793 the French Republic appointed Edmond Charles Genêt, familiarly called "Citizen Genêt," Minister to the United States. He was a young man, not more than thirty, of very quick parts, who had been brought up in the Bureau of Foreign Affairs, had an exorbitant idea of his own importance, and might be described without malice as a master of effrontery. The ship which brought him to this country was driven by adverse winds to Charleston and landed him there on April 8th. He lost no time in fitting out a privateer against British mercantile vessels. The fact that by so doing he broke the American rule of neutrality did not seem to trouble him at all; on the contrary, he acted as if he were simply doing what the United States would do if they really did what they wished. As soon as he had made his arrangements, he proceeded by land up the coast to Philadelphia. Jefferson was exuberant, and he wrote in exultation to Madison on the fifth of May, concluding with the phrase, "I wish we may be able to repress the spirit of the people within the limits of a fair neutrality." If there be such things as crocodile tears, perhaps there may also be crocodile wishes, of which this would seem to be one. A friend of Hamilton's, writing about the same time, speaks in different terms, as follows:

He has a good person, a fine ruddy complexion, quite active, and seems always in a bustle, more like a busy man than a man of business. A Frenchman in his manners, he announces himself in all companies as the Minister of the Republic, etc., talks freely of his commission, and, like most Europeans, seems to have adopted mistaken notions of the penetration and knowledge of the people of the United States. His system, I think, is to laugh us into war if he can.[1]

Citizen Genêt did not allow his progress up the coast to be so rapid that he was deprived of any ovation. The banquets, luncheons, speech-makings, by which he was welcomed everywhere, had had no parallel in the country up to that time. They seemed to be too carefully prepared to be unpremeditated, and probably many of those who took part in them did not understand that they were cheering for a cause which they had never espoused. One wonders why he was allowed to carry on this personal campaign and to show rude unconcern for good manners, or indeed for any manners except those of a wayward and headstrong boy. It might be thought that the Secretary of State abetted him and in his infatuation

[1] Irving, v, 151.

for France did not check him; but, so far as I have discovered, no evidence exists that Jefferson was in collusion with the truculent and impertinent "Citizen." No doubt, however, the shrewd American politician took satisfaction in observing the extravagances of his fellow countrymen in paying tribute to the representative of France. At Philadelphia, for instance, the city which already was beginning to have a reputation for spinster propriety which became its boast in the next century, we hear that ". . . before Genêt had presented his credentials and been acknowledged by the President, he was invited to a grand republican dinner, 'at which,' we are told, 'the company united in singing the Marseillaise Hymn. A deputation of French sailors presented themselves, and were received by the guests with the fraternal embrace.' The table was decorated with the 'tree of liberty,' and a red cap, called the cap of liberty, was placed on the head of the minister, and from his travelled in succession from head to head round the table." [1]

But not all the Americans were delirious enthusiasts. Hamilton kept his head amid the whirling words which, he said, might "do us much harm and could do France no good." In a letter, which deserves to be quoted in spite of its length, he states very clearly

[1] Jay's *Life*, 1, 30.

the opinions of one of the sanest of Americans. He
writes to a friend:

It cannot be without danger and inconvenience to our
interests, to impress on the nations of Europe an idea
that we are actuated by the same spirit which has for
some time past fatally misguided the measures of those
who conduct the affairs of France, and sullied a cause
once glorious, and that might have been triumphant.
The cause of France is compared with that of America
during its late revolution. Would to Heaven that the comparison were just! Would to Heaven we could discern,
in the mirror of French affairs, the same decorum, the
same gravity, the same order, the same dignity, the
same solemnity, which distinguished the cause of the
American Revolution! Clouds and darkness would not
then rest upon the issue as they now do. I own I do not
like the comparison. When I contemplate the horrid
and systematic massacres of the 2nd and 3rd of September, when I observe that a Marat and a Robespierre,
the notorious prompters of those bloody scenes, sit tri-
umphantly in the convention, and take a conspicuous
part in its measures — that an attempt to bring the
assassins to justice has been obliged to be abandoned —
when I see an unfortunate prince, whose reign was a continued demonstration of the goodness and benevolence
of his heart, of his attachment to the people of whom he
was the monarch, who, though educated in the lap of
despotism, had given repeated proofs that he was not
the enemy of liberty, brought precipitately and ignominiously to the block without any substantial proof of
guilt, as yet disclosed — without even an authentic exhibition of motives, in decent regard to the opinions of
mankind; when I find the doctrine of atheism openly
advanced in the convention, and heard with loud ap-
plause; when I see the sword of fanaticism extended to

force a political creed upon citizens who were invited to submit to the arms of France as the harbingers of liberty; when I behold the hand of rapacity outstretched to prostrate and ravish the monuments of religious worship, erected by those citizens and their ancestors; when I perceive passion, tumult, and violence usurping those seats, where reason and cool deliberation ought to preside, I acknowledge that I am glad to believe there is no real resemblance between what was the cause of America and what is the cause of France; that the difference is no less great than that between liberty and licentiousness. I regret whatever has a tendency to confound them, and I feel anxious, as an American, that the ebullitions of inconsiderate men among us may not tend to involve our reputation in the issue.[1]

Citizen Genêt continued his campaign unabashed. He attempted to force the United States to give arms and munitions to the French. Receiving cool answers to his demands, he lost patience, and intended to appeal to the American People, over the head of the Government. He sent his communication for the two Houses of Congress, in care of the Secretary of State, to be delivered. But Washington, whose patience had seemed inexhaustible, believed that the time had come to act boldly. By his instruction Jefferson returned the communication to Genêt with a note in which he curtly reminded the obstreperous Frenchman of a diplomat's proper behavior. As the American Government had already requested

---

[1] *Hamilton's Works*, 566.

the French to recall Genêt, his amazing inflation collapsed like a pricked bladder. He was too wary, however, to return to France which he had served so devotedly. He preferred to remain in this country, to become an American citizen, and to marry the daughter of Governor Clinton of New York. Perhaps he had time for leisure, during the anticlimax of his career, to recognize that President Washington, whom he had looked down upon as a novice in diplomacy, knew how to accomplish his purpose, very quietly, but effectually. A century and a quarter later, another foreigner, the German Ambassador, Count Bernstorff, was allowed by the American Government to weave an even more menacing plot, but the sound sense of the country awoke in time to sweep him and his truculence and his conspiracies beyond the Atlantic.

The intrigues of Genêt emphasized the fact that a party had arisen and was not afraid to speak openly against President Washington. He held in theory a position above that of parties, but the theory did not go closely with fact, for he made no concealment of his fundamental Federalism, and every one saw that, in spite of his formal neutrality, in great matters he almost always sided with Hamilton instead of with Jefferson. When he himself recognized that the rift was spreading between his two chief Cabinet officers, he warned them both to avoid exaggerating their differences and pursuing any policy which must be harmful to the country. Patriotism was the chief aim of every one, and patriotism meant sinking one's private desires in order to achieve liberty through unity. Washington himself was a man of such strict virtue that he could work with men who in many matters disagreed with him, and as he left the points of disagreement on one side, he used the more effectively points of agreement. I do not think that Jefferson could do this, or Hamilton either, and I cannot rid myself of the suspicion that Jefferson furnished Philip Freneau, who came from New York to Philadelphia to edit the anti-Washington newspaper, with much of his inspiration if not actual articles. The objective of the "Gazette" was, of course, the destruction of Hamilton and his policy of finance. If Hamilton could be thus destroyed, it would be far easier to pull down Washington also. Lest the invectives in the "Gazette" should fail to shake Washington in his regard for Hamilton, Jefferson indited a serious criticism of the Treasury, and he took pains to have friends of his leave copies of the indictment so that Washington could not fail to see them. The latter, however, by a perfectly natural and characteristic stroke which Jefferson could not foresee, sent the indictment to Hamilton and asked him to explain.

This Hamilton did straightforwardly and point-blank — and Jefferson had the mortification of perceiving that his ruse had failed. Hamilton, under a thin disguise, wrote a series of newspaper assaults on Jefferson, who could not parry them or answer them. He was no match for the most terrible controversialist in America; but he could wince. And presently B. F. Bache, the grandson of Benjamin Franklin, brought his unusual talents in vituperation, in calumny, and in nastiness to the "Aurora," a blackguard sheet of Philadelphia. Washington doubtless thought himself so hardened to abuse by the experience he had had of it during the Revolution that nothing which Freneau, Bache, and their kind could say or do, would affect him. But he was mistaken. And one cannot fail to see that they saddened and annoyed him. He felt so keenly the evil which must come from the deliberate sowing of dissensions. He cared little what they might say against himself, but he cared immensely for their sin against patriotism. Before his term as President drew to a close, he was already deciding not to be a candidate for a second term. He told his intention to a few intimates — from them it spread to many others. His best friends were amazed. They foresaw great trials for the Nation and a possible revolution. Hamilton tried to move him by every sort of appeal. Jefferson

also was almost boisterous in denouncing the very
idea. He impressed upon him the importance of his
continuing at that crisis. He had not been President
long enough to establish precedents for the new
Nation. There were many volatile incidents which,
if treated with less judgment than his, might do
grievous harm. One wonders how sincere all the en-
treaties to Washington were, but one cannot doubt
that the great majority of the country was perfectly
sincere in wishing to have him continue; for it had
sunk deep into the hearts of Americans that Washington was himself a party, a policy, an ideal above
all the rest. And when the election was held in the
autumn of 1792, he was reëlected by the equivalent
of a unanimous vote.

CHAPTER X

THE JAY TREATY

THERE is no doubt that Washington in his Olympian quiet took a real satisfaction in his election. On January 20, 1793, he wrote to Governor Henry Lee of Virginia:

A mind must be insensible indeed not to be gratefully impressed by so distinguished and honorable a testimony of public approbation and confidence; and as I suffered my name to be contemplated on this occasion, it is more than probable that I should, for a moment, have experienced chagrin, if my reëlection had not been by a pretty respectable vote. But to say I feel pleasure from the prospect of commencing another term of duty would be a departure from the truth, — for, however it might savor of affectation in the opinion of the world (who, by the by, can only guess at my sentiments, as it never has been troubled with them), my particular and confidential friends well know, that it was after a long and painful conflict in my own breast, that I was withheld, (by considerations which are not necessary to be mentioned), from requesting in time, that no vote might be thrown away upon me, it being my fixed determination to return to the walks of private life at the end of my term.[1]

Washington felt at his reëlection not merely egotistic pleasure for a personal success, but the assur-

[1] Ford, XII, 256.

ance that it involved a triumph of measures which he held to be of far more importance than any success of his own. The American Nation's new organism which he had set in motion could now continue with the uniformity of its policy undisturbed by dislocating checks and interruptions. Much, very much depended upon the persons appointed to direct its progress, and they depended upon the President who appointed them. In matters of controversy or dispute, Washington upheld a perfectly impartial attitude. But he did not believe that this should shackle his freedom in appointing. According to him a man must profess right views in order to be considered worthy of appointment. The result of this was that Washington's appointees must be orthodox in his definition of orthodoxy.

His first important act in his new administration was to issue a Proclamation of Neutrality on April 22d. Although this document was clear in intent and in purpose, and was evidently framed to keep the United States from being involved in the war between France and England, it gave offence to partisans of either country. They used it as a weapon for attacking the Government, so that Washington found to his sorrow that the partisan spites, which he had hoped would vanish almost of their own accord, were become, on the contrary, even more for-

midable and irritating. At this juncture the coming
of Genêt and his machinations added greatly to
the embarrassment, and, having no sense of decency,
Genêt insinuated that the President had usurped
the powers of Congress and that he himself would
seek redress by appealing to the people over the
President. I have already stated that, having tolerated Genêt's insults and menaces as far as he deemed
necessary, Washington put forth his hand and
crushed the spluttering Frenchman like a bubble.

Persons who like to trace the sardonic element in
history — the element which seems to laugh deri-
sively at the ineffectual efforts of us poor mortals to
establish ourselves and lead rational lives in the world
as it is — can find few better examples of it than these
early years of the American Republic. In the war
which brought about the independence of the American Colonies, England had been their enemy and
France their friend. Now their instinctive gratitude
to France induced many, perhaps a majority of them,
to look with effusive favor on France, although her
character and purpose had quite changed and it was
very evident that for the Americans to side with
France would be against sound policy and common
sense. Neutrality, the strictest neutrality, between
England and France was therefore the only rational
course; but the American partisans of these rivals

did their utmost to render this unachievable. Much of Washington's second term see-sawed between one horn and the other of this dilemma. The sardonic aspect becomes more glaring if we remember that the United States were a new-born nation which ought to have been devoting itself to establishing viable relations among its own population and not to have been dissipating its strength taking sides with neighbors who lived four thousand miles away.

In the autumn of 1793 Jefferson insisted upon resigning as Secretary of State. Washington used all his persuasiveness to dissuade him, but in vain. Jefferson saw the matter in its true light, and insisted. Perhaps it at last occurred to him, as it must occur to every dispassionate critic, that he could not go on forever acting as an important member of an administration which pursued a policy diametrically opposed to his own. After all, even the most adroit politicians must sometimes sacrifice an offering to candor, not to say honesty. At the end of the year he retired to the privacy of his home at Monticello, where he remained in seclusion, not wholly innocuous, until the end of 1796. Edmund Randolph succeeded him as Secretary of State.

Whether it was owing to the departure of Jefferson from the Cabinet or not, the fact remains that Washington concluded shortly thereafter the most difficult diplomatic negotiation of his career. This was the treaty with England, commonly called Jay's Treaty. The President wished at first to appoint Hamilton, the ablest member of the Cabinet, but, realizing that it would be unwise to deprive himself and his administration of so necessary a supporter, he offered the post to John Jay, the Chief Justice of the Supreme Court. The quality, deemed most desirable, which it was feared Jay might lack, was audacity. But he had discretion, tact, and urbanity in full share, besides that indefinable something which went with his being a great gentleman.

The President, writing to Gouverneur Morris, who had recently been recalled as Minister to France, said:

My primary objects, to which I have steadily adhered, have been to preserve the country in peace, if I can, and to be prepared for war if I cannot, to effect the first, upon terms consistent with the respect which is due to ourselves, and with honor, justice and good faith to all the world.

Mr. Jay (and not Mr. Jefferson) as has been suggested to you, embarked as envoy extraordinary for England about the middle of May. If he succeed, well; if he does not, why, knowing the worst, we must take measures accordingly.[1]

Jay reached London early in June, 1794, and labored over the treaty with the British negotiators

[1] Ford, XII, 436. Mount Vernon, June 25, 1794.

during the summer and autumn, started for home before Christmas, and put the finished document in Washington's hands in March. From the moment of his going enemies of all kinds talked bitterly against him. The result must be a foregone conclusion, since John Jay was regarded as the chief Anglomaniac in America after Hamilton. They therefore condemned in advance any treaty he might agree to. But their criticism went deeper than mere hatred of him: it sprang from an inveterate hatred of England, which dated from before the Revolution. Since the Treaty of 1783 the English seemed to act deliberately with studied truculence, as if the Americans would not and could not retaliate. They were believed to be instigating the Indians to continuous underhand war. They had reached that dangerous stage of truculence, when they did not think it mattered whether they spoke with common diplomatic reticence. Lord Dorchester, the Governor-General of Canada, and to-day better known as Sir Guy Carleton, his name before they made him a peer, addressed a gathering of Indian chiefs at Quebec on the assumption that war would come in a few weeks. President Washington kept steady watch of every symptom, and he knew that it would not require a large spark to kindle a conflagration. "My objects are, to prevent a war," he wrote to Edmund Randolph, on April 15, 1794, "if justice can be obtained by fair and strong representations (to be made by a special envoy) of the injuries which this country has sustained from Great Britain in various ways, to put it into a complete state of military defence, and to provide *eventually* for such measures as seem to be now pending in Congress for execution, if negotiations in a reasonable time proves unsuccessful." [1]

The year 1794 marked the sleepless anxiety of the Silent President. Day and night his thoughts were in London, with Jay. He said little; he had few letters from Jay — it then required from eight to ten weeks for the mail clippers to make a voyage across the Atlantic. Opposition to the general idea of such a treaty as the mass of Republicans and Anti-Federalists supposed Washington hoped to secure, grew week by week. The Silent Man heard the cavil and said nothing.

At last early in 1795 Jay returned. His Treaty caused an uproar. The hottest of his enemies found an easy explanation on the ground that he was a traitor. Stanch Federalists suffered all varieties of mortification. Washington himself entered into no discussion, but he ruminated over those which came to him. I am not sure that he invented the phrase "Either the Treaty, or war," which summed up the

[1] Ford, XIII, 4-9.

alternatives which confronted Jay; but he used it
with convincing emphasis. When it came before the
Senate, both sides had gathered every available
supporter, and the vote showed only a majority of
one in its favor. Still, it passed. But that did not
satisfy its pertinacious enemies. Neither were they
restrained by the President's proclamation. The
Constitution assigned the duty of negotiating and
ratifying treaties to the President and Senate; but
to the perfervid Anti-Britishers the Constitution
was no more than an old cobweb to be brushed away
at pleasure. The Jay Treaty could not be put into
effect without money for expenses; all bills involving
money must pass the House of Representatives;
therefore, the House would actually control the operation of the Treaty.

The House at this time was Republican by a marked
majority. In March, 1796, the President laid the
matter before the House. In a twinkling the flood-
gates of speechifying burst open; the debates touched
every aspect of the question. James Madison, the
wise supporter of Washington and Hamilton in
earlier days and the fellow worker on "The Federalist," led the Democrats in their furious attacks.
He was ably seconded by Albert Gallatin, the high-
minded young Swiss doctrinaire from Geneva, a
terrible man, in whose head principles became two-

edged weapons with Calvinistic precision and mer-
cilessness. The Democrats requested the President
to let them see the correspondence in reference to the
Treaty during its preparation. This he wisely declined to do. The Constitution did not recognize
their right to make the demand, and he foresaw that,
if granted by him then, it might be used as a harmful precedent.

For many weeks the controversy waxed hot in the
House. Scores of speakers hammered at every argu-
ment, yet only one speech eclipsed all the rest, and
remains now, after one hundred and thirty years, a
paragon. There are historians who assert that this
was the greatest speech delivered in Congress before
Daniel Webster spoke there — an implication which
might lead irreverent critics to whisper that too much
reading may have dulled their discrimination. But
fortunately not only the text of the speech remains;
we have also ample evidence of the effect it produced
on its hearers. Fisher Ames, a Representative from
Massachusetts, uttered it. He was a young lawyer,
feeble in health, but burning, after the manner of
some consumptives, with intellectual and moral fire
which strangely belied his slender thread of physical
life. Ames pictured the horrors which would ensue if
the Treaty were rejected. Quite naturally he assumed
the part of a man on the verge of the grave, which

increased the impressiveness of his words. He spoke
for three hours. The members of the House listened
with feverish attention; the crowds in the balconies
could not smother their emotion. One witness reports that Vice-President John Adams sat in the
gallery, the tears running down his cheeks, and that
he said to the friend beside him, "My God, how
great he is!"

When Ames began, no doubt the Anti-British
groups which swelled the audience turned towards
him an unsympathetic if not a scornful attention —
they had already taken a poll of their members, from
which it appeared that they could count on a majority of six to defeat the Treaty. As he proceeded,
however, and they observed how deeply he was
moving the audience, they may have had to keep up
their courage by reflecting that speeches in Congress
rarely change votes. They are intended to be read
by the public outside, which is not under the spell of
the orator or the crowd. But when Fisher Ames,
after what must have seemed to them a whirlwind
speech, closed with these solemn, restrained words,
they must have doubted whether their victory was
won:

Even the minutes I have spent in expostulating, have
their value [he said] because they protract the crisis and
the short period in which alone we may resolve to escape

it. Yet I have, perhaps, as little personal interest in the event as any one here. There is, I believe, no member, who will not think his chance to be a witness of the consequences greater than mine. If, however, the vote should pass to reject — even I, slender and almost broken as my hold on life is, may outlive the government and Constitution of my country.[1]

The next day when the vote was taken it appeared that the Republicans, instead of winning by a majority of six, had lost by three.

The person who really triumphed was George Washington, although Fisher Ames, who won the immediate victory, deserved undying laurel. The Treaty had all the objections that its critics brought against it then, but it had one sterling virtue which outweighed them all. It not only made peace between the United States and Great Britain the normal condition, but it removed the likelihood that the wrangling over petty matters might lead to war. For many years Washington had a fixed idea that if the new country could live for twenty years without a conflict with its chief neighbors, its future would be safe; for he felt that at the end of that time it would have grown so strong by the natural increase in population and by the strength that comes from developing its resources, that it need not fear the attack of any people in the world. The Jay Treaty

[1] Elson, 359.

helped towards this end; it prevented war for sixteen years only; but even that delay was of great service to the Americans and made them more ready to face it than they would have been in 1795.

CHAPTER XI

WASHINGTON RETIRES FROM PUBLIC LIFE

THE Treaty with England had scarely been put in operation before the Treaty with France, of which Washington also felt the importance, came to the front. Monroe was not an aggressive agent. Perhaps very few civilized Americans could have filled that position to the satisfaction of his American countrymen. They wished the French to acknowledge and explain various acts which they qualified as outrages, whereas the French regarded as glories what they called grievances. The men of the Directory which now ruled France did not profess the atrocious methods of the Terrorists, but they could not afford in treating with a foreigner to disavow the Terrorists. In the summer of '96, Washington, being dissatisfied with Monroe's results, recalled him, and sent in his place Charles Cotesworth Pinckney, to whom President Adams afterwards added John Marshall and Elbridge Gerry, forming a Commission of three. Some of the President's critics have regarded his treatment of Monroe as unfair, and they imply that it was inspired by partisanship. He had always been an undisguised Federalist, whereas Monroe, during the past year or more, had followed Jefferson and become an unswerving Democrat. The publication here of a copy of Monroe's letter to the French Committee of Public Safety caused a sensation; for he had asserted that he was not instructed to ask for the repeal of the French decrees by which the spoliation of American commerce had been practised, and he added that if the decrees benefited France, the United States would submit not only with patience but with pleasure. What wonder that Washington, in reading this letter and taking in the full enormity of Monroe's words, should have allowed himself the exclamation, "Extraordinary!" What wonder that in due course of time he recalled Monroe from Paris and replaced him with a man whom he could trust!

The settlement of affairs with France did not come until after Washington ceased to be President. I will, therefore, say no more about it, except to refer to the outrageous conduct of the French, who hurried two of the Commissioners out of France, and, apparently at the instigation of Talleyrand, declared that they must pay a great deal of money before they made any arrangement, to which Charles Pinckney made the famous rejoinder, "Millions for defence, but not one cent for tribute." The negotiations became so stormy that war seemed imminent.

Congress authorized President Adams to enlist ten thousand men to be put into the field in case of need, and he wrote to Washington: "We must have your name, if you will in any case permit us to use it. There will be more efficacy in it than in many an army." McHenry, the Secretary of War, wrote: "You see how the storm thickens, and that our vessel will soon require its ancient pilot. Will you — may we flatter ourselves, that in a crisis so awful and important, you will accept the command of all our armies? I hope you will, because you alone can unite all hearts and all hands, if it is possible that they can be united." [1]

To President Adams Washington replied on July 4, 1799: "As my whole life has been dedicated to my country in one shape or another, for the poor remains of it, it is not an object to contend for ease and quiet, when all that is valuable is at stake, further than to be satisfied that the sacrifice I should make of these, is acceptable and desired by my country." [2]

Congress voted to restore for Washington the rank of Commander-in-Chief, and he agreed with the Secretary of War that the three Major-Generals should be Alexander Hamilton, Inspector-General; Charles C. Pinckney, who was still in Europe; and Henry Knox. But a change came over the passions

[1] Irving, v, 290.   [2] *Ibid.*, 291.

of France; Napoleon Bonaparte, the new despot who had taken control of that hysterical republic for himself, was now aspiring to something higher and larger than the humiliation of the United States and his menace in that direction ceased.

We need to note two or three events before Washington's term ended because they were thoroughly characteristic. First of these was the Whiskey Insurrection in western Pennsylvania. The inhabitants first grew surly, then broke out in insurrection on account of the Excise Law. They found it cheaper to convert their corn and grain into whiskey, which could be more easily transported, but the Government insisted that the Excise Law, being a law, should be obeyed. The malcontents held a great mass meeting on Braddock's Field, denounced the law and declared that they would not obey it. Washington issued a proclamation calling upon the people to resume their peaceable life. He called also on the Governors of Pennsylvania, Maryland, New Jersey, and Virginia for troops, which they furnished. His right-hand lieutenant was Alexander Hamilton, who felt quite as keenly as he did himself the importance of putting down such an insurrection. Washington knew that if any body of the people were allowed unpunished to rise and disobey any law which pinched or irritated them, all law and order would very soon go by

from blame. To him, the magnanimous President replied in part:

If I had entertained any suspicions before, that the queries, which have been published in Bache's paper, proceeded from you, the assurances you have given of the contrary would have removed them; but the truth is, I harbored none. I am at no loss to *conjecture* from what source they flowed, through what channel they were conveyed, and for what purpose they and similar publications appear. They were known to be in the hands of Mr. Parker in the early part of the last session of Congress. They were shown about by Mr. Giles during the session, and they made their public exhibition about the close of it.

Perceiving and probably hearing, that no abuse in the gazettes would induce me to take notice of anonymous publications against me, those, who were disposed to do me *such friendly offices*, have embraced without restraint every opportunity to weaken the confidence of the people; and, by having the whole game in their hands, they have scrupled not to publish things that do not, as well as those which do exist, and to mutilate the latter, so as to make them subserve the purposes which they have in view.[1]

Washington's opinion of the scurrilous crusade against him, he expressed in the following letter to Henry Lee:

But in what will this abuse terminate? For the result, as it respects myself, I care not; for I have a consolation within that no earthly efforts can deprive me of, and that is, that neither ambition nor interested motives have influenced my conduct. The arrows of malevo-

[1] Ford, XIII, 229.

lence, therefore, however barbed and well pointed, never can reach the most vulnerable part of me; though, whilst I am up as a mark, they will be continually aimed. The publications in Freneau's and Bache's papers are outrages in that style in proportion as their pieces are treated with contempt and are passed by in silence by those at whom they are aimed. The tendency of them, however, is too obvious to be mistaken by men of cool and dispassionate minds, and, in my opinion, ought to alarm them, because it is difficult to prescribe bounds to the effect.[1]

By his refusal to take notice of these indecencies, Washington set a high example. In other countries, in France and England, for example, the victims of such abuse resorted to duels with their abusers: a very foolish and inadequate practice, since it happened as often as not that the aggrieved person was killed. In taking no notice of the calumnies, therefore, Washington prevented the President of the United States from being drawn into an unseemly duel. We cannot fail to recognize also that Washington was very sensitive to the maintenance of freedom of speech. He seems to have acted on the belief that it was better that occasionally license should degenerate into abuse than that liberty should be suppressed. He was the President of the first government in the world which did not control the utterances of its people. Perhaps he may have

1 Lodge, II, 236.

supposed that their patriotism would restrain them from excesses, and there can be no doubt that the insane gibes of the Freneaus and the Baches gave him much pain because they proved that those scorpions were not up to the level which the new Nation offered them.

As the time for the conclusion of Washington's second term drew near, he left no doubt as to his intentions. Though some of his best friends urged him to stand for reëlection, he firmly declined. He felt that he had done enough for his country in sacrificing the last eight years to it. He had seen it through its formative period, and had, he thought, steered it into clear, quiet water, so that there was no threatening danger to demand his continuance at the helm. Many persons thought that he was more than glad to be relieved of the increasing abuse of the scurrilous editors. No doubt he was, but we can hardly agree that merely for the sake of that relief he would abandon his Presidential post. But does it not seem more likely that his unwillingness to convert the Presidency into a life office, and so to give the critics of the American experiment a valid cause for opposition, led him to establish the precedent that two terms were enough? More than once in the century and a quarter since he retired in 1797, over-ambitious Presidents have schemed to win a third election and flattering sycophants have encouraged them to believe that they could attain it. But before they came to the test Washington's example — "no more than two" — has blocked their advance. In this respect also we must admit that he looked far into the future and saw what would be best for posterity. The second term as it has proved is bad enough, diverting a President during his first term to devote much of his energy and attention to setting traps to secure the second. It might be better to have only one term to last six years, instead of four, which would enable a President to give all his time to the duties of his office, instead of giving a large part of it to the chase after a reëlection.

As soon as Washington determined irrevocably to retire, he began thinking of the "Farewell Address" which he desired to deliver to his countrymen as the best legacy he could bequeath. Several years before he had talked it over with Madison, with whom he was then on very friendly terms, and Madison had drafted a good deal of it. Now he turned to Hamilton, giving him the topics as far as they had been outlined, and bidding him to rewrite it if he thought it desirable. In September, 1796, Washington read the "Address" before the assembled Congress.

The "Farewell Address" belongs among the few

supreme utterances on human government. Its author seems to be completely detached from all personal or local interests. He tries to see the thing as it is, and as it is likely to be in its American environment. His advice applies directly to the American people, and only in so far as what he says has in a large sense human pertinence do we find in it more than a local application.

"Be united" is the summary and inspiration of the entire "Address." "Be united and be American"; as an individual each person must feel himself most strongly an American. He urges against the poisonous effects of parties. He warns against the evils that may arise when parties choose different foreign nations for their favorites.

The great rule of conduct for us [he says] in regard to foreign Nations is, in extending our commercial relations, to have with them as little *Political* connection as possible. So far as we have already formed engagements, let them be fulfilled with perfect good faith. Here let us stop.

Europe has a set of primary interests, which to us have none, or a very remote relation. Hence she must be engaged in frequent controversies, the causes of which are essentially foreign to our concerns. Hence, therefore, it must be unwise in us to implicate ourselves by artificial ties in the ordinary vicissitudes of her politics, . . . or enmities.

Our detached and distant situation invites and enables us to pursue a different course. If we remain one

People, under an efficient government, the period is not far off, when we may defy material injury from external annoyance; when we may take such an attitude as will cause the neutrality we may at any time resolve upon to be scrupulously respected. When belligerent nations, under the impossibility of making acquisitions upon us, will not lightly hazard the giving us provocation when we may choose peace or war, as our interest guided by justice shall counsel.

Why forego the advantages of so peculiar a situation? Why quit our own to stand upon foreign ground? Why, by interweaving our destiny with that of any part of Europe, entangle our peace and prosperity in the toils of European ambition, rivalship, interest, humour or caprice?

Compared with Machiavelli's "Prince," which must come to the mind of every one who reads the "Farewell Address," one sees at once that the "Prince" is more limber, it may be more spontaneous, but the great difference between the two is in their fundamental conception. The "Address" is frankly a preachment and much of its impressiveness comes from that fact. The "Prince," on the other hand, has little concern with the moral aspect of politics discussed and makes no pretence of condemning immoral practices or making itself a champion of virtue. In other words, Washington addresses an audience which had passed through the Puritan Revolution, while Machiavelli spoke to men who were familiar with the ideals and crimes of the Italian Renaissance.

Washington spread his gospel so clearly that all persons were sure to learn and inwardly digest it, and many of them assented to it in their minds, although they did not follow it in their conduct. His paramount exhortations — "Be united" — "Be Americans"; "do not be drawn into complications with foreign powers" — at times had a very real living pertinence. The only doctrine which still causes controversy is that which touches our attitude towards foreign countries. During the late World War we heard it revived, and a great many persons who had never read the "Farewell Address" gravely reminded us of Washington's warning against "entangling alliances." As a matter of fact, that phrase does not appear in the "Farewell Address" at all. It was first used by Thomas Jefferson in his first Inaugural Address, March 4, 1801, sixteen months after Washington was dead and buried. No doubt the meaning could be deduced from what Washington said in more than one passage of his "Farewell." But to understand in 1914 what he said or implied in 1796, we must be historical. In 1796 the country was torn by conflicting parties for and against strong friendship, if not an actual alliance, between the United States on one side and Great Britain or France on the other. Any foreign alliance that could be made in 1914, however, could not have been, for the same reason, with either Great Britain or France. The aim proposed by its advocates was to curb and destroy the German domination of the world. Now Washington was almost if not quite the most actual of modern statesmen. All his arrangements at a given moment were directed at the needs and likelihood of the moment, and in 1914 he would have planned as 1914 demanded. He would have steered his ship by the wind that blew then and not by the wind that had blown and vanished one hundred and twenty years before.

Some one has remarked that, while Washington achieved a great victory in the ratification of the Jay Treaty, that event broke up the Federalist Party. That is probably inexact, but the break-up of the Federalist Party was taking place during the last years of Washington's second administration. The changes in Washington's Cabinet were most significant, especially as they nearly all meant the change from a more important to a less important Secretary. Thus John Jay, the first Secretary of State, really only an incumbent *ad interim*, gave way to Thomas Jefferson, who was replaced by Edmund Randolph in 1794, and who in turn was succeeded by Timothy Pickering in 1795. Alexander Hamilton was Secretary of the Treasury from the beginning in 1789 to 1795, when he made way for Oliver Wolcott, Jr.

Henry Knox, the original Secretary of War, was succeeded by Timothy Pickering in 1795, who, after less than a year, was followed by James McHenry. Edmund Randolph served as Attorney-General in 1789 to 1794, then retiring for William Bradford who, after a brief year, was replaced by Charles Lee. The Postmaster-Generalship was filled from 1789 to 1791 by Samuel Osgood, and then by Timothy Pickering. Thus at the end of Washington's eight years we find that in the place of two really eminent men, like Jefferson and Hamilton, he was served by Edmund Randolph and Oliver Wolcott, Jr., and James McHenry, good routine men at the best, mediocrities if judged by comparison with their predecessors. Moreover, the reputation for discretion of some of them, suffered. Thus Randolph had not long been Secretary of State when Joseph Fauchet, the French Minister, produced some papers which could be construed as implying that Randolph had accepted money. Randolph was known to be impecunious, but his personal honor had never been suspected. Washington with characteristic candor sent Randolph the batch of incriminating letters. Randolph protested that he "forgave" the President and tried to exculpate himself in the newspapers. Even that process of deflation did not suffice and he had recourse to a "Vindication," which was read by few and popularly believed to vindicate nobody. Washington is believed to have held Randolph as guiltless, but as weak and as indiscreet. He pitied the ignominy, for Randolph had been in a way Washington's protégé, whose career had much interested him and whose downfall for such a cause was doubly poignant.

CHAPTER XII

CONCLUSION

WASHINGTON'S term as President ended at noon on March 4, 1797. He was present at the inauguration of President John Adams which immediately followed. On the 3d, besides attending to the final necessary routine, he wrote several letters of farewell to his immediate friends, including Henry Knox, Jonathan Trumbull, Timothy Pickering, and James McHenry. To all he expressed his grief at personal parting, but also immense relief and happiness in concluding his public career. He said, for instance, in his letter to Trumbull:

Although I shall resign the chair of government without a single regret, or any desire to intermeddle in politics again, yet there are many of my compatriots, among whom be assured I place you, from whom I shall part sorrowing; because, unless I meet with them at Mount Vernon, it is not likely that I shall ever see them more, as I do not expect that I shall ever be twenty miles from it, after I am tranquilly settled there. To tell you how glad I should be to see you at that place is unnecessary. To this I will add that it would not only give me pleasure, but pleasure also to Mrs. Washington, and others of the family with whom you are acquainted, and who all unite, in every good wish for you and yours.[1]

[1] Ford, XIII, 377.

In a few days he returned to Mount Vernon and there indulged himself in a leisurely survey of the plantation. He rode from one farm to another and reacquainted himself with the localities where the various crops were either already springing or would soon be. Indoors there was an immense volume of correspondence to be attended to with the aid of Tobias Lear, the faithful secretary who had lived with the President during the New York and Philadelphia periods. When the letters were sorted, many answers had to be written, some of which Washington dictated and others he wrote with his own hand. He admits to Secretary McHenry that, when he goes to his writing table to acknowledge the letters he has received, when the lights are brought, he feels tired and disinclined to do this work, conceiving that the next night will do as well. "The next night comes," he adds, "and with it the same causes for postponement, and so on." He has not had time to look into a book. He is dazed by the incessant number of new faces which appear at Mount Vernon. They come, he says, out of "respect" for him, but their real reason is curiosity. He practises Virginian hospitality very lavishly, but he cannot endure the late hours. So he invites his nephew, Lawrence Lewis, to spend as much time as he can at Mount Vernon while he himself and Mrs. Washington go to

bed early, "soon after candle light." Lewis accepted
the invitation all the more willingly because he found
at the mansion Nelly Custis, a pretty and sprightly
young lady with whom he promptly fell in love and
married later. Nelly and her brother George had
been adopted by Washington and brought up in the
family. She was his particular pet. Like other mature men he found the boys of the younger generation somewhat embarrassing. I suppose they felt, as
well they might, a great and awful gulf yawning between them. "I can govern men," he would say,
"but I cannot govern boys." [1] With Nelly Custis,
however, he found it easy to be chums. No one can
forget the mock-serious letter in which he wrote to
her in regard to becoming engaged and gave her advice about falling in love. The letter is unexpected
and yet it bears every mark of sincerity and reveals
a genuine vein in his nature. We must always think
of Nelly as one of the refreshments of his older life
and as one of its great delights. He considered himself an old man now. His hair no longer needed
powder; years and cares had made it white. He
spoke of himself without affectation as a very old
man, and apparently he often thought, as he was
engaged in some work, "this is the last time I shall
do this." He seems to have taken it for granted that

[1] Irving, v, 277.

he was not to live long; but this neither slackened his industry nor made him gloomy. And he had in truth spent a life of almost unremitting laboriousness. Those early years as surveyor and Indian fighter and pathfinder were years of great hardships. The eight years of the Revolution were a continuous physical strain, an unending responsibility, and sometimes a bodily deprivation. And finally his last service as President had brought him disgusts, pinpricks which probably wore more on his spirits than did the direct blows of his opponents. Very likely he felt old in his heart of hearts, much older than his superb physical form betokened. We cannot but rejoice that Nelly Custis flashed some of the joyfulness and divine insouciance of youth into the tired heart of the tired great man.

Perhaps the best offhand description of Washington in these later days is that given by an English actor, Bernard, who happened to be driving near Mount Vernon when a carriage containing a man and a woman was upset. Bernard dismounted to give help, and presently another rider came up and joined in the work. "He was a tall, erect, well-made man, evidently advanced in years, but who appeared to have retained all the vigor and elasticity resulting from a life of temperance and exercise. His dress was a blue coat buttoned to the chin, and buckskin

FAMILY GROUP AT MOUNT VERNON

By Edward Savage

breeches." [1] They righted the chaise, harnessed the horse, and revived the young woman who, true to her time and place, had fainted. Then she and her companion drove off towards Alexandria. Washington invited Bernard to come home with him and rest during the heat of the day. The actor consented. From what the actor subsequently wrote about that chance meeting I take the following paragraphs, some of which strike to the quick:

In conversation his face had not much variety of expression. A look of thoughtfulness was given by the compression of the mouth and the indentations of the brow (suggesting an habitual conflict with, and mastery over, passion), which did not seem so much to disdain a sympathy with trivialities as to be incapable of denoting them. Nor had his voice, so far as I could discover in our quiet talk, much change or richness of intonation, but he always spoke with earnestness, and his eyes (glorious conductors of the light within) burned with a steady fire which no one could mistake for mere affability; they were one grand expression of the well-known line: "I am a man, and interested in all that concerns humanity." In one hour and a half's conversation he touched on every topic that I brought before him with an even current of good sense, if he embellished it with little wit or verbal elegance. He spoke like a man who had felt as much as he had reflected, more than he had spoken; like one who had looked upon society rather in the mass than in detail, and who regarded the happiness of America but as the first link in a series of universal victories; for his full faith in the power of those re-

[1] Lodge, II, 277.

sults of civil liberty which he saw all around him led him to foresee that it would erelong, prevail in other countries and that the social millennium of Europe would usher in the political. When I mentioned to him the difference I perceived between the inhabitants of New England and of the Southern States, he remarked: "I esteem those people greatly, they are the stamina of the Union and its greatest benefactors. They are continually spreading themselves too, to settle and enlighten less favored quarters. Dr. Franklin is a New Englander." When I remarked that his observations were flattering to my country, he replied, with great good humor, "Yes, yes, Mr. Bernard, but I consider your country the cradle of free principles, not their armchair. Liberty in England is a sort of idol; people are bred up in the belief and love of it, but see little of its doings. They walk about freely, but then it is between high walls; and the error of its government was in supposing that after a portion of their subjects had crossed the sea to live upon a common, they would permit their friends at home to build up those walls about them." [1]

We find among the allusions of several strangers who travelled in Virginia in Washington's later days, who saw him or perhaps even stayed at Mount Vernon, some which are not complimentary. More than one story implies that he was a hard taskmaster, not only with the negroes, but with the whites. Some of the writers go out of their way to pick up unpleasant things. For instance, during his absence from home a mason plastered some of the rooms, and when Wash-

[1] Lodge, II, 338, 339.

ington returned he found the work had been badly done, and remonstrated. The mason died. His widow married another mason, who advertised that he would pay all claims against his forerunner. Thereupon Washington put in a claim for fifteen shillings, which was paid. Washington's detractors used this as a strong proof of his harshness. But they do not inform us whether the man was unable to pay, or whether the claim was dishonest. Since the man paid voluntarily and did not question the rightness of the amount, may we not at least infer that he had no quarrel? And if he had not, who else had?

Insinuations concerning Washington's lack of sympathy for his slaves was a form which in later days most of the references to his care of them took. But here also there are evident facts to be taken into account. The Abolitionists very naturally were prejudiced against every slave-owner; they were also prejudiced in favor of every slave. Washington, on the contrary, harbored no prepossessions for or against the black man. He found the slaves idle, incompetent, lazy, although he would not have denied that the very fact of slavery caused and increased these evils. He treated the negroes justly, but without any sentimentality. He found them in the order in which he lived. They were the workmen

of his plantation; he provided them with food, clothing, and a lodging; in return they were expected to
give him their labor. It does not appear that the
slaves on Washington's plantation endured any
special hardship. A physician attended them at their
master's expense when they were sick. That he
obliged them to do their specified work, that he
punished them in case of dishonesty, just as he
would have done to white workmen, were facts
which he never would have thought a rational person
would have regarded as heinous. In his will he freed
his slaves, not for the Abolitionist's reason, but because he regarded slavery as the most pernicious
form of labor, debasing alike the slave and his master, uneconomic and most wasteful.

But in so general a matter as Washington's treatment of his slaves, we must be careful not to take a
solitary case and argue from it as if it were habitual.
By common report his slaves were so well treated
that they regretted it if there was talk of transferring
them to other planters. We have many instances
cited which show his unusual kindness. When he
found, for instance, that a mulatto woman, who had
lived many years with one of the negroes, had been
transferred to another part of his domain and that
the negro pined for her, he arranged to have her
brought back so that they might pass their old age

together. The old negro was his servant, Billy Lee, who suffered an accident to his knee, which made him a cripple for the rest of his life. This he spent at Mount Vernon well cared for. Washington continued to the end the old custom of supplying a hogshead of rum for the negroes to drink at harvest time, always premising that they must partake of it sparingly.

Washington's religious beliefs and practices have also occasioned much controversy. If we accept his own statements at their plain value, we must regard him as a Church of England man. I do not discover that he was in any sense an ardent believer. He preferred to say "Providence" rather than "God," probably because it was less definite. He attended divine service on Sundays, whenever a church was near, but for a considerable period at one part of his life he did not attend communion. He thoroughly believed in the good which came from church-going in the army and he always arranged to have a service on Sundays during his campaigns. When at Mount Vernon, on days when he did not go out to the service, he spent several hours alone in meditation in his study. The religious precepts which he had been taught in childhood remained strong in him through life. He believed moral truths, and belief with him meant putting in practice what he professed. While he had imbibed much of the deistic spirit of the middle of the eighteenth century it would be inaccurate to infer that he was not fundamentally a Christian.

After Washington withdrew to Mount Vernon, early in the spring of 1797, his time was chiefly devoted to agriculture and the renewing of his life as a planter. He declined all public undertakings except that which President Adams begged him to assume — the supreme command of the army in case of the expected war with France. That new duty undoubtedly was good for him, for it proved to him that at least all his official relations with the Government had not ceased, and it also served to cheer the people of the country to know that in case of military trouble their old commander would lead them once more. Washington gave so much attention to this work, which could be in the earlier stages arranged at Mount Vernon, that he felt justified in accepting part of the salary which the President allotted to him. But the war did not come. As Washington prophesied, the French thought better of their truculence. The new genius who was ruling France had in mind something more grandiose than a war with the American Republic.

On December 10, 1799, Washington sent a long letter to James Anderson in regard to agricultural plans for his farm during the year 1800. He calculates closely the probable profits, and specifies the rotation of crops on five hundred and twenty-five acres. The next day, December 12th, he wrote a short note to Alexander Hamilton, in regard to the organization of a National Military Academy, a matter in which the President had long been deeply interested. The day was stormy. "Morning snowing and about three inches drop. Wind at Northeast, and mercury at 30. Continued snowing till one o'clock, and about four it became perfectly clear. Wind in the same place, but not hard. Mercury 28 at night." Washington, who scorned to take any account of weather, rode for five hours during the morning to several of the farms on his plantations, examining the conditions at each and conferring with the overseers.

On reaching home he complained a little of chilliness. His secretary, Tobias Lear, observed that he feared he had got wet, but Washington protested that his greatcoat had kept him dry; in spite of which the observant Lear saw snow hanging to his hair and remarked that his neck was wet. Washington went in to dinner, which was waiting, without changing his dress, as he usually did. "In the evening he appeared as well as usual. The next day, Friday, there was a heavy fall of snow, but having a severe cold, he went out for only a little while to mark some trees, between the house and the river which were to be cut down. During the day his hoarseness increased, but he made light of it, and paid no heed to the suggestion that he should take something for it, only replying, as was his custom, that he would 'let it go as it came.'"

Mrs. Washington went upstairs to a room on the floor above to chat with Mrs. Lewis (Nelly Custis) who had recently been confined. Washington remained in the parlor with Lear, and when the evening mail was brought in from the post-office, they read the newspapers; Washington even reading aloud, as well as his sore throat would allow, anything "which he thought diverting or interesting." Then Lear read the debates of the Virginia Assembly on the election of a Senator and Governor. "On hearing Mr. Madison's observations respecting Mr. Monroe, he appeared much affected, and spoke with some degree of asperity on the subject, which I endeavored to moderate," says Lear, "as I always did on such occasions. On his returning to bed, he appeared to be in perfect health, excepting the cold before mentioned, which he considered as trifling, and had been remarkably cheerful all the evening."

At between two and three o'clock of Saturday morning, December 14th, Washington awoke Mrs. Washington and told her that he was very unwell and had had an ague. She observed that he could hardly speak and breathed with difficulty. She wished to get up to call a servant, but he, fearing she might take cold, dissuaded her. When daylight appeared, the woman Caroline came and lighted the fire. Mrs. Washington sent her to summon Mr. Lear, and Washington asked that Mr. Rawlins, one of the overseers, should be summoned before the Doctor could arrive. Lear got up at once, dressed hastily, and went to the General's bedside. Lear wrote a letter to Dr. Craik, Washington's long-time friend and physician, and sent it off post-haste by a servant. Mrs. Washington was up. They prepared a mixture of molasses, vinegar, and butter, but the patient could not swallow a drop; whenever he attempted it he appeared to be distressed, convulsed, and almost suffocated.

"Mr. Rawlins came in soon after sunrise and prepared to bleed him. When the arm was ready, the General, observing that Rawlins appeared to be agitated, said, as well as he could speak, 'Don't be afraid,' and after the incision was made, he observed, 'The orifice is not large enough.' However, the blood ran pretty freely. Mrs. Washington, not knowing whether bleeding was proper or not in the General's situation, begged that much might not be taken from him, lest it should be injurious, and desired me to stop it; but when I was about to untie the string, the General put up his hand to prevent it, and as soon as he could speak, he said, 'More.' Mrs. Washington being still very uneasy, lest too much blood should be taken, it was stopped after about half a pint was taken from him.

"Finding that no relief was obtained from bleeding, and that nothing would go down the throat, I proposed bathing the throat externally with salvolatile which was done; during the operation, which was with the hand, in the gentlest manner, he observed, ''T is very sore.' A piece of flannel dipped in salvolatile was then put round his neck. His feet were also bathed in warm water. This, however, gave no relief. In the meantime, before Dr. Craik arrived, Mrs. Washington requested me to send for Dr. Brown, of Port Tobacco, whom Dr. Craik had recommended to be called, if any case should ever occur that was seriously alarming. I despatched a Messenger (Cyrus) to Dr. Brown immediately (between eight and nine o'clock). Dr. Craik came in soon after, and after examining the General, he put a blister of Cantharide on the throat and took some more blood from him, and had some Vinegar and hot water put into a Teapot for the General to draw in the steam from the nozel, which he did as well as he was able. He also ordered sage tea and Vinegar to be mixed for a Gargle. This the General used as often as desired; but when he held back his head to let it run down, it put him into great distress and almost produced suffocation. When the mixture came out of his mouth some phlegm followed it, and he would attempt to cough, which the Doctor encouraged him to do as much as he could; but without effect — he could only make the attempt.

"About eleven o'clock, Dr. Dick was sent for. Dr. Craik requested that Dr. Dick might be sent for, as he feared Dr. Brown would not come in time. A message was accordingly despatched for him. Dr. Craik bled the General again about this time. No effect, however, was produced by it, and he continued in the same state, unable to swallow anything. Dr. Dick came in about three o'clock, and Dr. Brown arrived soon after. Upon Dr. Dick's seeing the General, and consulting a few minutes with Dr. Craik, he was bled gain, the blood ran very slowly and did not produce any symptoms of fainting. Dr. Brown came into the chamber room soon after, and upon feeling the General's pulse &c., the Physicians went out together. Dr. Craik soon after returned. The General could now swallow a little — about four o'clock Calomel and tartar emetic were administered; but without any effect. About half past four o'clock, he desired me to ask Mrs. Wash-

ington to come to his bedside — when he requested
her to go down into his room and take from his desk
two wills which she would find there, and bring them
to him, which she did. Upon looking at them he
gave her one, which he observed was useless, as it
was superseded by the other, and desired her to burn
it, which she did, and then took the other and put it
away into her closet. After this was done, I returned again to his bedside and took his hand. He
said to me, 'I find I am going, my breath cannot
continue long; I believed from the first attack it
would be fatal — do you arrange and record all my
late military letters and papers — arrange my accounts and settle my books, as you know more
about them than any one else, and let Mr. Rawlins
finish recording my other letters.' He then asked if
I recollected anything which it was essential for him
to do, as he had but a very short time to continue
with us. I told him that I could recollect nothing,
but that I hoped he was not so near his end. He observed, smiling, that he certainly was, and that, as
it was the debt which we all must pay, he looked to
the event with perfect resignation.

"In the course of the afternoon he appeared to be in
great pain and distress, from the difficulty of breathing, and frequently changed his posture in the bed.
On these occasions I lay upon the bed and endeav-

ored to raise him, and turn him with as much ease as possible. He appeared penetrated with gratitude for my attentions, and often said, 'I am afraid I shall fatigue you too much'; and upon my answering him, that I could feel nothing but a wish to give him ease, he replied, 'Well, it is a debt we must pay to each other, and I hope, when you want aid of this kind, you will find it.' He asked when Mr. Lewis and Washington [1] would return. They were then in New Kent. I told him I believed about the 20th of the month. He made no reply.

"About five o'clock Dr. Craik came again into the room, and upon going to the bedside the General said to him: 'Doctor, I die hard, but I am not afraid to go. I believed, from my first attack, that I should not survive it. My breath cannot last long.' The Doctor pressed his hand, but could not utter a word. He retired from the bedside, and sat by the fire absorbed in grief. The physicians, Dr. Dick and Dr. Brown, again came in (between five and six o'clock), and when they came to his bedside, Dr. Craik asked him if he could sit up in the bed. He held out his hand to me and was raised up, when he said to the Physicians: 'I feel myself going. I thank you for your attention — you had better not take any more trouble about me; but let me go off quietly; I cannot

[1] George Washington Parke Custis.

last long.' They found out that all which had been done was of no effect. He lay down again, and all retired except Dr. Craik. He continued in the same position, uneasy and restless, but without complaining; frequently asking what hour it was. When I helped to move him at this, he did not speak, but looked at me with strong expressions of gratitude. The Doctor pressed his hand, but could not utter a word. He retired from the bedside, and sat by the fire absorbed in grief. About eight o'clock the Physicians came again into the Room and applied blisters, and cataplasms of wheat bran, to his legs and feet: but went out (except Dr. Craik) without a ray of hope. I went out about this time, and wrote a line to Mr. Low and Mr. Peter requesting them to come with their wives (Mrs. Washington's granddaughters) as soon as possible.

"From this time he appeared to breathe with less difficulty than he had done; but was very restless, constantly changing his position to endeavor to get ease. I aided him all in my power, and was gratified in believing he felt it: for he would look upon me with his eyes speaking gratitude; but unable to utter a word without great distress. About ten o'clock he made several attempts to speak to me before he could effect it. At length, he said: 'I am just going. Have me decently buried, and do not let my body be put into the Vault in less than three days after I am dead.' I bowed assent, for I could not speak. He then looked at me again, and said, 'Do you understand me?' I replied, 'Yes, sir.'

"''T is well,' said he. About ten minutes before he expired his breathing became much easier; he lay quietly; he withdrew his hand from mine and felt his own pulse. I spoke to Dr. Craik who sat by the fire; he came to the bedside. The General's hand fell from his wrist. I took it in mine and laid it upon my breast. Dr. Craik put his hand on his eyes and he expired without a struggle or a Sigh! While we were fixed in silent grief, Mrs. Washington, who was sitting at the foot of the bed, asked, with a firm and collected voice, 'Is he gone?' I could not speak, but held up my hand as a signal that he was. ''T is well,' said she in a plain voice. 'All is now over. I have no more trials to pass through. I shall soon follow him.'" [1]

Once read, honest Tobias Lear's account of Washington's death will hardly be forgotten. It has a majestic simplicity which we feel must have accompanied Washington in his last hours. The homely sick-bed details; his grim fortitude; his willingness to do everything which the physicians recommended,

---

[1] Ford, XIV, 246–52. I have copied Tobias Lear's remarkable account of Washington's death almost verbatim.

not because he wanted to live, nor because he thought they would help him, but because he wished to obey. We see him there trying to force out the painful words from his constricted throat and when he was unable to whisper even a "thank you" for some service done, Lear read the unuttered gratitude in his eyes. The faithful Lear, lying on the outside of the bed in order to be able to help turn Washington with less pain, and poor old Dr. Craik, lifelong friend, who became too moved to speak, so that he sat off near the fire in silence except for a stifled sob, and Mrs. Washington, placed near the foot of the bed, waiting patiently in complete self-control. She seemed to have determined that the last look which her mate of forty years had of her should not portray helpless grief. And from time to time the negro slaves came to the door that led into the entry and they peered into the room very reverently, and with their emotions held in check, at their dying master. And then there was a ceasing of the pain and the breathing became easier and quieter and Dr. Craik placed his hand over the life-tired eyes and Washington was dead without a struggle or even a sigh.

The pathos or tragedy of it lies in the fact that all the devices and experiments of the doctors could avail nothing. The quinsy sore throat which killed him could not be cured by any means then known to medical art. The practice of bleeding, which by many persons was thought to have killed him, was then so widely used that his doctors would have been censured if they had omitted it. Sixty years later it was still in use, and no one can doubt that it deprived Italy's great statesman of his chance of living. The premonition of Washington on his first seizure with the quinsy that the end had come proved fatally true.

The news of Washington's death did not reach the capital until Wednesday, December 18th. The House immediately adjourned. On the following day, when it reassembled, John Marshall delivered a brief tribute and resolutions were passed to attend the funeral and to pay honor "to the memory of the Man, first in war, first in peace, and first in the hearts of his countrymen." The immortal phrase was by Colonel Henry Lee, the father of General Robert E. Lee. President Adams, in response to a letter from the Senate of the United States, used the less happy phrase, "If a Trajan found a Pliny, a Marcus Aurelius can never want biographers, eulogists, or historians."

During the days immediately following Washington's death, preparations were made at Mount Vernon for the funeral. They sent to Alexandria for a coffin and Dr. Dick measured the body, which he found to be exactly six feet three and one half inches in length. The family vault was on the slope of the hill, a little to the south of the house. Mrs. Washington desired that a door should be made for the vault instead of having it closed up as formerly, after the body should be deposited, observing that "it will soon be necessary to open it again." Mourning clothes were prepared for the family and servants. The ceremony took place on Wednesday. There were many troops. Eleven pieces of artillery were brought down from Alexandria and a schooner belonging to Mr. R. Hamilton came down and lay off Mount Vernon to fire minute guns. The pall-holders were Colonels Little, Charles Sims, Payne, Gilpin, Ramsay, and Marsteller, and Colonel Blackburne walked before the corpse. Colonel Deneal marched with the military. About three o'clock the procession began to move. Colonels Little, Sims and Deneal and Dr. Dick directed the arrangements of the procession. This moved out through the gate at the left wing of the house and proceeded around in front of the lawn and down to the vault on the right wing of the house. The procession was as follows: The troops; horse and foot; music playing a solemn dirge with muffled drums; the clergy, viz.: the Reverends Mr. Davis, Mr. James Miner, and Mr. Moffatt, and

Mr. Addison; the General's horse, with his saddle, holsters, and pistols, led by two grooms, Cyrus and Wilson, in black; the body borne by officers and Masons who insisted upon carrying it to the grave; the principal mourners, viz.: Mrs. Stuart and Mrs. Low, Misses Nancy and Sally Stuart, Miss Fairfax, and Miss Dennison, Mr. Low and Mr. Peter, Dr. Craik and T. Lear; Lord Fairfax and Ferdinando Fairfax; Lodge No. 23; Corporation of Alexandria. All other persons, preceded by Mr. Anderson, Mr. Rawlins, the Overseers, etc., etc.

The Reverend Mr. Davis read the service and made a short extempore speech. The Masons performed their ceremonies and the body was deposited in the vault. All then returned to the house and partook of some refreshment, and dispersed with the greatest good order and regularity. The remains of the provisions were distributed among the blacks. Mr. Peter, Dr. Craik, and Dr. Thornton tarried here all night.[1]

The Committee appointed by Congress to plan a suitable memorial for Washington proposed a monument to be erected in the city of Washington, to be adorned with statuary symbolizing his career as General and as President, and containing a tomb for himself and for Mrs. Washington. The latter replied

[1] From notes by T. Lear, Ford, XIV, 254-55.

to President Adams that "taught by the great example which I have so long had before me, never to
oppose my private wishes to the public will, I must
consent to the request made by Congress, which you
have had the goodness to transmit me, and in doing
this, I need not say, I cannot say, what a sacrifice of
individual feeling I make to a sense of public duty."
The intended monument at the capital was never
erected. Martha Washington lies beside her husband where she wished to be, in the family vault at
Mount Vernon. From her chamber window in the
upper story of the Mount Vernon house she could
look across the field to the vault. She died in 1802,
a woman of rare discretion and good sense who, during forty years, proved herself the worthiest companion of the founder of his country.

I have wished to write this biography of George
Washington so that it would explain itself. There is
no need of eulogy. All eulogy is superfluous. We see
the young Virginia boy, born in aristocratic conditions, with but a meagre education, but trained by
the sports and rural occupations of his home in perfect manliness, in courage, in self-reliance, in resourcefulness. Some one instilled into him moral
precepts which fastened upon his young conscience
and would not let him go. At twenty he was phys-

ically a young giant capable of enduring any hardship and of meeting any foe. He ran his surveyor's chain far into the wilderness to the west of Mount Vernon. When hardly a man in age, the State of Virginia knew of his qualities and made him an officer in its militia. At only twenty-three he was invited to accompany General Braddock's staff, but neither he nor angels from heaven could prevent Braddock from plunging with typical British bullheadedness into the fatal Indian ambush. He gave up border warfare, but did not cease to condemn the inadequacy of the Virginia military equipment and its training. He devoted himself to the pursuits of a large planter, and on being elected a Burgess, he attended regularly the sessions at Williamsburg. Wild conditions which in his boyhood had reached almost to Fauquier County, had drifted rapidly westward. Within less than ten years of Braddock's defeat, Fort Duquesne had become permanently English and the name of Pittsburgh reminded men of the great British statesman who had urged on the fateful British encroachment on the Ohio River. For Washington in person, the lasting effect of the early training and fighting in western Pennsylvania was that it gave him direct knowledge of the Indian and his ways, and that it turned his imagination to thinking out the problem of developing the Middle West, and of keeping the connections between the East and the West strong and open.

In the House of Burgesses Washington was a taciturn member, yet he seemed to have got a great deal of political knowledge and wisdom so that his colleagues thought of him as the solid man of the House and they referred many matters to him as if for final decision. He followed political affairs in the newspapers. Above all, at Mount Vernon he heard all sides from the guests who passed his domain and enjoyed his hospitality. From the moment that the irritation between Great Britain and the Colonies became bitter he seems to have made up his mind that the contention of the Colonists was just. After that he never wavered, but he was not a sudden or a shallow clamorer for Independence. He believed that the sober second sense of the British would lead them to perceive that they had made a mistake. When at length the Colonies had to provide themselves with an army and to undertake a war, he was the only candidate seriously considered for General, although John Hancock, who had made his peacock way so successfully in many walks of life, thought that he alone was worthy of the position. Who shall describe Washington's life as Commander-in-Chief of the Colonial forces during the Revolutionary War? What other commander ever had a task like his?

For a few weeks the troops led by Napoleon — the barefooted and ragged heroes of Lodi and Arcola and Marengo — were equally destitute, but victory brought them food and clothes and prosperity. Whereas Washington's men had no comfort before victory and none after it.

Some of the military critics to-day deny Washington's right to be ranked among the great military commanders of the world, but the truth is that he commanded during nearly eight years and won one of the supreme crucial wars of history against far superior forces. The General who did that was no understrapper. The man whose courage diffused itself among the ten thousand starving soldiers at Valley Forge, and enabled them to endure against the starvation and distress of a winter, may very well fail to be classified among the Prince Ruperts and the Marshal Neys of battle, but he ranks first in a higher class. His Fabian policy, which troubled so many of his contemporaries, saved the American Revolution. His title as General is secure. Nor should we forget that it was his scrupulous patriotism which prevented the cropping out of militarism in this country.

Finally, a country which owed its existence to him chose him to be for eight years its first President. He saw the planting of the roots of the chief organs of its government. In every act he looked far forward into the future. He shunned making or following evil precedents. He endured the most virulent personal abuse that has ever been poured out on American public men, preferring that to using the power which his position gave him, and denaturing the President into a tyrant. Nor should we fail to honor him for his insistence on dignity and a proper respect for his office. His enemies sneered at him for that, but we see plainly how much it meant to this new Nation to have such qualities exemplified. Had Thomas Jefferson been our first President in his *sans-culotte* days, our Government might not have outlasted the *sans-culottist* enthusiasts in France. A man is known by his friends. The chosen friends of Washington were among the best of his time in America. Hamilton, Henry Knox, Nathanael Greene, John Jay, John Marshall — these were some.

Although Washington was less learned than many of the men of his time in political theory and history, he excelled them all in a concrete application of principles. He had the widest acquaintance among men of different sorts. He heard all opinions, but never sacrificed his own. As I have said earlier, he was the most *actual* statesman of his time; the people in Virginia came very early to regard him as a man apart;

this was true of the later days when the Government sat in New York and Philadelphia. If they sought a reason, they usually agreed that Washington excelled by his character, and if you analyze most closely you will never get deeper than that. Reserved he was, and not a loose or glib talker, but he always showed his interest and gave close attention. After Yorktown, when the United States proclaimed to the world that they were an independent Republic, Europe recognized that this was indeed a Republic unlike all those which had preceded it during antiquity and the Middle Age. Foreigners doubted that it could exist. They doubted that Democracy could ever govern a nation. They knew despots, like the Prussian King, Frederic, who walked about the streets of Berlin and used his walking-stick on the cringing persons whom he passed on the sidewalk and did not like the looks of. They remembered the crazy Czar, Peter, and they knew about the insane tendencies of the British sovereign, George. The world argued from these and other examples that monarchy was safe; it could not doubt that the supply of monarchs would never give out; but it had no hope of a Republic governed by a President. It was George Washington more than any other agency who made the world change its mind and conclude that the best President was the best kind of monarch.

It is reported that after he died many persons who had been his neighbors and acquaintances confessed that they had always felt a peculiar sense of being with a higher sort of person in his presence: a being not superhuman, but far above common men. That feeling will revive in the heart of any one to-day who reads wisely in the fourteen volumes of "Washington's Correspondence," in which, as in a mine, are buried the passions and emotions from which sprang the American Revolution and the American Constitution. That George Washington lived and achieved is the justification and hope of the United States.

THE END

INDEX

INDEX

Throughout the index, the initial *W.* is used for the name of George Washington.

47950   2058
             260ct'43   39201
   23 Jan'40   13Apr'6?

                 8561
             10 Mar'47
45377
             15212
   3 Mar'40   16 May'4?

40545   22701

   15   27Jan'51
62712   47351
   17 Jul'41
             24 Jun'57
54730
   15   '4?   X7609
             11Mar'59
10Mar'43   29396
   103?
22May 43   19Dec'6?